MIND SENSE

A PRACTICAL WORKBOOK

Mind Sense

Fine-Tuning Your
Intellect & Intuition

KATHLYN RHEA
with Josef Quattro

CELESTIAL ARTS
Berkeley, California

*My deepest gratitude to all the special people
around the world who wrote and called after reading
The Psychic Is You. May your intellect and intuition
become your most valued partners on the
path to a life filled with success.*

—KATHLYN RHEA

CELESTIAL ARTS
P.O. Box 7327
Berkeley, California 94707

Cover design by Ken Scott
Text design by Nancy Austin
Composition by Designer Type

Library of Congress Cataloging-in-Publication Data
Rhea, Kathlyn.
    Mind Sense: fine-tuning your intellect and intuition: a
practical workbook / Kathlyn Rhea with Josef Quattro.
      p.   cm.
    1. Intuition (Psychology)—Problems, exercises, etc. 2. Intuition
(Psychology) 3. Intellect. I. Quattro, Josef. II. Title.
BF311.R44 1988
153.4'4—dc19
ISBN 0-89087-529-4

First Printing, 1988

Manufactured in the United States of America

1 2 3 4 5 6 7 8 9 0 — 92 91 90 89 88

This book is dedicated to Leonard Albert Worthington, attorney-at-law. His life has been spent exploring the limitless potential of humanity and giving freely to thousands who needed his help along the way. He has cleared a path for many of us to follow.

Contents

The *American Heritage Dictionary* offers the following definitions:

intellect—the ability to learn and reason as distinguished from the ability to feel or will; capacity for knowledge and understanding.

intuition—the act or faculty of knowing without rational processes; immediate cognition

ONE

My Intuition

As a child I always had an intuitive sense of things. So strong was this sense that I often insisted on clinging to my own feelings about things, and Mother would accuse me of being hard-headed or stubborn. Many times I would state, "It doesn't matter what other people think; what matters is what feels right to me." Possibly one of the reasons my mother suffered from migraine headaches was because of her high sense of intuition, which she unfortunately didn't understand. Intuition can enhance your life if you understand it, but it can also make your life more difficult if you don't understand it!

My sense of knowing often caused sleepless nights for my parents as well as myself. I would lie awake at night, being aware of feelings in the room that hadn't been explained to me. Boy, did my parents ever hate that! Having been raised with the conventional wisdom that says that you can know only what parents and teachers have explained to you, these ambiguous feelings that drifted up to me as I relaxed before falling asleep created a fear in me. Many a night I tried to climb into bed with my parents because of that fear. They would carry me along the hallway to my room, turn on the lights, check under the bed and in the closet. They never saw anything—because those feelings came from something not identifiable by the other senses.

Fortunately, my father never seemed to find my actions unusual. I believe this was partly because he listened to his own intuition. The morning after a sleepless night, he would encourage me to understand how I felt about things.

After graduating from college with a bachelor of fine arts degree, I went into various fields without having had any previous experience in them. For example, I opened a number of modeling schools; had my own television show, hosted a women's radio show, wrote a news column, staged local and statewide Miss America pageants, built a teen club, taught at a correctional school for girls, and studied the role that intuition plays in life. Without any prior experience, in each endeavor I just *knew without question* that each was something I could do. It may seem I was bolder than others in taking chances, but really I was just following my gut feelings. I would actually play each role out in my head before taking it on, then know it so well that I only had to perform the task, just like an actor who knows the lines before going on stage.

After marrying a Navy fighter pilot, I settled in Norfolk, Virginia, where I decided to open my first modeling school. Three other modeling schools had already failed in the area, so many people told me it would be impossible to have one succeed. An editor at a local television station told me it was a bad idea—and even wished me all the bad luck in the world. My husband didn't think I could get a bank to help with the finances, and he gently advised me, "I would go to the bank with you, but I think you need to learn that this dream is an impossible one."

Well, the first thing I did was go out and look for a building. The one I found in the right location was a new brick building about to open. The workers finishing the interior told me that all the spaces had been filled. I *knew* that was the perfect location, so I met with the owner. After meeting with me and picking up the strong program I was broadcasting—the program that said that the building was the right one for me—he ended up feeling that he just had to give me that location.

At about the same time, I had seen a copy of *House Beautiful*. The leading interior decorator in that issue happened to live in Norfolk. Intuitively, I knew he was the person to do the interior. The school had to give people the impression of being well established—a permanent part of the community. I proceeded to sell my program to the decorator, to which he replied that he would be most happy to decorate the school for me at much below his normal rates.

The next trip was to the bank. And for the rest of my life, I will never forget Mr. Northern, who was one of the vice presidents of the bank. He looked like the man who played Santa Claus in *A Miracle on 42nd Street*—angelic, with snow white hair. His reply was, "Kay, we've never done anything like this before, and I don't know why I'm doing this, but we're going to back you." He did, even to the point of giving me free and detailed advice about interest and payments.

To this day, some thirty years later, Charm Associates is still in Norfolk, Virginia. All of this was accomplished to the amazement of my husband, who was used to plain facts and figures as a chemical engineer and as a Navy fighter pilot—facts and figures that in this case had seemed contrary to success.

My intuition was working back then, before I had ever studied it. My intuitive feeling told me I'd succeed. It convinced me, and I used that conviction to convince others.

During that time I found it interesting to toss around the concept of intuition at parties, to see how people reacted. Even though it was seldom mentioned back then, intelligent people were willing to talk about it. Nobody reacted as if it were absurd or incomprehensible, but they usually thought of it as a special gift, a special *something* that someone possessed—and that someone had to be a witch, or a fortune teller, or something of that nature.

There I was, looking for an understanding of intuition, and the only people I could turn to were those who read cards, palms, or crystal balls. All of them told me they were gifted with a "special power," something that God had given them. Well, I didn't feel that God had chosen me to be apart from everyone else. Believing there was more to it than that, I began asking them how this sense worked. Every one of them had a different story, and none of the stories matched. It was like asking several scientists how an atom breaks down, and each one of them positing a different theory. It was frustrating and made little sense to me.

As I progressed in my quest, I came to realize that none of these people really knew, so therefore they were telling me the story their mothers or someone else had given them. That's when it became obvious those people were not different from the rest of us. They had just been fed misinformation (a product of ignorance) along the way.

Fortunately, as I continued to investigate, I found doctors, ministers, scientists, and other educated people who were interested in working together with me on the role intuition plays within each of us. The more I counseled clients, the more I began deliberately looking for it in people and working with it. At first I gave people a few intuitive facts, which amazed them—and me too. As time went by I began to provide my clients with more information about themselves, the types of professions suitable for them, and facts about family relationships. With regular practice, my sense of intuition produced details that had not been obvious to my other five senses. I've found it useful in locating missing dogs, cats, horses, heirlooms, and children; selecting investment stocks; locating oil and gold mines; advising large corporations about hiring executives, partnerships that should or should not be formed, and whether products should be marketed and when; establishing security for heads of state; and solving hundreds of homicide cases. At first a few facts would amaze me, but then I began applying intuition to everything. It's just the same as anything else in life—the more you practice, the better you become.

I've found intuition to be as limitless as language. As a young child you use the letters of the alphabet merely to write your name and address. Later you may use them to write a thesis, novel, play, opera, or proposal for world peace. There is no limit to what you can do with the alphabet, as I have since discovered there is no limit to how you can apply your intuition once you recognize and exercise it.

An intelligent young medical doctor and his wife came to me in California, asking if I would help them learn to use their intuition. When I agreed, they let out sighs of relief and related how they had requested this from half a dozen other people. Those people had told this couple that God had to give them the gift, that no one could just learn to be intuitive. The reason they said this, of course, was because they did not have any more knowledge of the role intuition really played than this couple did. They had the native intuition, but lacked the intellect to explain how it worked. All of those people believed it was a gift.

As I said in *The Psychic Is You*, if it's a gift, which is something you are given freely, I certainly had to work many years to pay for mine! After twenty years of hard work, I feel like I've earned a Ph.D. in intuition, rather than had a gift bestowed on me.

During my first two years of investigating this intriguing sense, I was residing on the Mayport naval base in Florida while my husband spent most of his time aboard an aircraft carrier as executive officer. When he returned from sea, and I informed him of my studies, he was convinced his fellow officers would feel certain I had lost my mind. I remember an incident at the first party celebrating the ship's return. He couldn't find me in the living room among the other women, who were talking about raising children and the difficulties that had arisen during their husbands' long absences. When he finally located me, he found the captain and most of his fellow officers grouped around me in the kitchen while they asked me question after question about a topic they seemed to find as interesting as I did. He was also unaware that during the time he had been at sea, several other naval officers had been studying the subject of intuition with me, a subject he was certain came under the heading of *For Women Only.*

As my search continued I frequently heard people speak of "woman's intuition," as though women were the sole proprietors of that sense. Yet I was discovering that men were equally aware of their own intuitive experiences. Since I first began offering classes in 1972, professional men have come to make up the majority—70 to 75 percent—of my students. Men tend to view the course in the same way that they would any educational tool. Upon learning the basics of the subject, they methodically begin to put it to use in their business and personal lives. I consider the idea that intuition is strictly a woman's birthright to be a myth.

Let's examine the reason this sense in women has been accepted down through the years. For you to recognize your intuition, it takes the same amount of time you must spend interpreting what your eyes see or your ears hear. It requires the ability or time devoted to relax enough so that you are able to get in touch with this feeling from within, without it being overshadowed by responses of the other senses. In the past, women spent more time in this mode. While performing repetitious chores such as rocking a cradle, weaving cloth, and churning butter, they were able to reflect upon the messages sent forth from the intuitive level while men were carving new frontiers, using mostly their intellect. Thus a myth was born. Now that today's woman is just as busy as her male counterpart, she must actually remind herself to use the intuitive process.

Intuition is not peculiar to any group. Anyone or anything with feelings can utilize it. Animals have it. My Doberman, Kelly, knows whether she can come along when I'm leaving the house. I don't have to tell her. She just senses the situation and saves herself the trouble of getting up if the answer is No.

I'm irritated by the way some people misinform the public about intuition. They either do it out of ignorance, or they deliberately mislead people so that they can appear to be special.

For example, in one homicide case I worked on, the murder had taken place in Yosemite National Park. After the suspect had been located from my description, the detective asked me to sit in on the interrogation. Because the suspect lived in another district of California, the questioning was to take place in the local office. Upon arriving, one of the detectives from that precinct introduced me to a local psychic, from whom he'd previously taken a course. This woman had asked to join us in the interrogation room, but because I knew that I could be equally intuitive about picking up *her* program of thoughts about the suspect, I didn't want her in the room while I was working on the case.

The suspect was brought into the room, and he sat across the table from the detective and me. As the questions began, he fidgeted in his seat and continually shifted his eyes to me as I jotted notes and passed them to the detective. From reading the suspect's program, I would redirect the interrogation with messages to the detective such as, "Don't believe that one. Who drove the car? Had he known the victim before that night?" A couple of hours of continual questions, questions to which we seemed to already know the answers, kept the suspect on edge until we had the needed information to prove his guilt.

Upon completing the task, our detective host invited us to lunch with him and the local psychic. Following the introduction that morning, I had had a distinct feeling that I would neither care to spend time in her company nor share her views or interpretations of her work. I felt her to be a publicity seeker and one whose intellect was less than average. This was confirmed during lunch, when I heard her casually say to the other detective, "I'm so tired today. I was out of my body all night helping people, and I'm just worn out." Had I ever made a statement of that nature to any of the hundreds of detectives I've worked with, they would have packed their briefcases, shaken their heads, and left my office. She was another one who didn't understand her intuition, so she made up statements to impress people.

On another occasion I was at a dinner party in the home of

friends attached to the German embassy. It was there I met a well-known psychic from Washington, D.C. Knowing she was Catholic, and walking a very thin line regarding how the church felt about her type of work, I got to talking with her, and asked, "How do you think it happens?" She replied, "Oh, I don't do it myself. God does it whenever he sees fit to give me a message." I asked, "Well, suppose that on Wednesday a person comes to you really needing help. If God hasn't spoken to you that day, what do you do?" She answered, "I just can't help that person."

Come on, I thought, if we have any intuition and intellect whatsoever, we don't have to wait for God to hand us the envelope with the answer. What I loved most about her was that God's envelopes always contained information about famous people. Was it so she could get famous in return? I've often wondered why he never gave her information about the everyday people that lived around her.

These people misrepresent their native intuition by calling it a power—a gift—and blanket their ignorance with accessories. Intuition has much more to it than that. It affects every decision you make, whether you listen to the right answer or ignore it and act out the wrong one.

Recently I saw the yearly headline of a certain tabloid promising predictions by "famous psychics" for the coming year. This has long been a source of annoyance to me. Being psychic is just being intuitive. We all have an intuitive sense, so these people have no more reason to be considered famous than anyone else. And why do they feel they have the right to intuitively look into anyone's closet? They'll tell you whether a leading actress is going to divorce her husband, what famous person is going to create a scandal, and what politician is going to become ill or die. These psychics make public predictions only to make themselves more famous, and I believe no one has the right to intuitively look into someone else's life without permission from that person. I have upset more than one television host because I refused to look into famous lives while on their shows. My scruples are the same when a parent comes to me about a grown-up offspring. I will not give the parent private information about a daughter or son without specific permission from the offspring. The same applies between a husband and wife, business partners, friends, and so on.

If I had my way, counselors in this field would have to earn a degree. They would have to pass a state board exam not unlike many professions require prior to practicing. I've known many psychologists and psychiatrists who have decided the working knowledge of intuition is a most important addition to a successful practice. I feel someday we will see the integration of it, particularly in counseling fields. Some universities already offer courses and degrees in parapsychology. With increased knowledge of this sense, it must continue to grow in effectiveness.

Dr. Russell Targ and Dr. Harold Puthoff, authors of *Mind Reach* (New York: Delacorte Press/E. Friede, 1977) and scientists at the Stanford Research Institute of Parapsychology, invited me to join a group in discussing how I blended law enforcement and intuition. Dr. Targ has the look of a man dedicated to science. He has a thick mane of hair that makes one think of Einstein. His intellect is as great as his sensitivity. He is a tall man, and appears totally unaware that his pants are a little too short. He wears glasses with thick lenses, and clasps his hands together while talking or listening. Having delved deeply into the research of parapsychology, he frequently looks off into space, putting his other senses aside to allow his feelings to surface.

When we had a break in conversation, he tipped forward onto the edge of his chair and said to me, "That's all very interesting. But what do you do in real life, Kay?" Having been under the impression that his years of research on ESP and my counseling *were* real life, I could not contain my laughter.

As I have counseled and spoken with scholars in the field, it has become apparent that intuition is as accessible as our other five senses and affects everything in a person's life. It affects the way we react to the world, the way we select our mates, and the way we select our jobs. If suppressed or ignored, it causes all kinds of emotional and physical stress, as well as many mistakes.

I believe that if you can see it, touch it, taste it, hear it, smell it, and make it work, then it's usable. And if it's not usable, it's really not worth much. That's why, upon discovering that intuition was a normal, everyday occurrence, I set forth to gain more knowledge on the subject, and then shared what I had discovered by writing my first book, *The Psychic Is You*, and now *Mind Sense*.

One thing to remember about this sense—it's just like your other senses. If you close your eyes, you may not see where you're going, and you'll fall down. If you close your ears, you may not hear directions, and you'll get lost. In the same way, you have to pay attention to your intuitive message. People that counsel in the field, such as myself, are not infallible. We also can ignore incoming programs and then pay the consequences.

One time I had an appointment to have my hair done. While brushing my hair and getting ready for bed the night before, I had a definite feeling of, "I don't really think I want to go and do this." Then my conscious mind overpowered it with previous training by my mother. "You can't be that inconsiderate. This man has marked off three hours in his book, first thing in the morning. You can't get in touch with him now. He won't be able to fill it up with clients. You can't do that to him." So I thought, "Okay. I really must go."

The next morning I was brushing my hair and getting ready for my day when the same thought occurred about not wanting to go. Once more, the good-little-girl training overpowered me with, "Come on. You can't leave this poor guy hanging." Well, I marched myself down to the salon, sat myself in the chair, and let him put all sorts of different things on my hair. Within two days the top of my head was nothing but blisters, and all of the hair on top of my head had fallen out. Not only was I bald, but I actually had second-degree burns on my scalp! Permanent scars now remind me that I'm not infallible, only human.

The entire time my intuition had said, "Don't go down there and get this done to yourself!" This story surprises people, because they always assume that I have all the answers in this field. I don't have any more answers than you do, unless I take the time to relax, interpret, and translate what my feelings are telling me.

A few years ago, I realized how difficult it was to be sure that detectives interpreted my words accurately. I discovered the importance of their needing to see the same exact picture I was seeing. After finding they heard my words and then came up with a mental picture that was only a rough approximation of what I meant concerning the appearance of the suspect, I began working with an artist, Tom Macris, of San Jose, California, who drew the face as I described it to him. Tom Macris is both an artist and a police officer, with a strong sense of intuition. With the two of us working together, we could hand a drawing of a face to the detectives. The first few attempts took most of two hours. Eventually we were able to finish a drawing of what the suspect looked like in my mind within thirty or forty minutes. Now we've had enough cases where the suspect or mug shot has matched the drawing that we realize it offers something of value. Twenty years ago, I never would have dreamed my intuition could provide that information, and I still feel I have just scratched the surface of what intuition can accomplish.

Some scientists work in the field of parapsychology, but others scoff at it. They're trying to tell me I can't do what I've done hundreds of times. How could I possibly imagine the face of a person who committed a crime when the detectives don't know who it is, the person has not been caught, and may live in another part of the country? How could I come up with all that information unless my intuition is at work?

It was Alexander Graham Bell who said he didn't question what he'd done until after the scientists came along and told him he couldn't do what he had already done.

TWO

Your Intuition & Intellect

*H*ave you ever thought about a friend in a far off place and then found a letter from that person waiting in your mailbox? Or picked up the phone to hear that person on the line? Did your amazement lead you to believe the situation was unusual?

Often someone will say to me, "You know, I suddenly thought of this person I hadn't seen in years, and then she called me. How unusual!"

And I say, "No, how *usual*. The fact that she was going to call *should* have made you think of her." Intuition is *usual*. It's one of the most usual things we do!

It's a basic sense that has always been there. It belongs to everyone. You have it! And like the other senses you use every day, it needs to be educated so you can apply it effectively.

All the best athletes, artists, lawyers, doctors, engineers, and detectives—and *you*—use intuition all the time, even if you don't know it. Albert Einstein said his theory of relativity came not only from his years of studying mathematics and his years of research, but also—and mainly—from his intuition. Hotel magnate Conrad Hilton told people to give him all the computed facts they wanted on a business deal, but if his intuition, his gut feeling, said, Don't buy, he would not go through with it. Einstein and Hilton had educated their sixth sense. Or was it their first sense?

Humanity actually used this sense first, even before language evolved, because it meant survival. It's the sense that suddenly knows to avoid an impending accident. In the night it alerts you to danger before it happens. Think about the American Indians. It was nothing for them to sit down and figure out what kind of winter they were going to have, so they would know where to move for food. Intuition was used as a basic tool for survival. As civilization began taking shape, they designated one person, a medicine man or woman, to tap that intuitive information in order to figure out what was best for the tribe, while everyone else went about using their other five senses for daily chores. Over the centuries this selected person began using intuition as if it were a power only he or she possessed, building a mystique around it so that the average person believed it was unique. The masses forgot that intuitive feeling was their natural heritage too.

Intuition is a basic, natural thing that has been neglected in people. All normal, healthy children are born with it. They *just know*, until we tell them they can't know unless they have learned it from parents, teachers, books, or others. They are constantly getting As or pats on the back for becoming what parents and educators think they should become. They're never getting praise for intuition, so their minds become crowded with things for which they receive credit. Pretty soon they've forgotten this way of knowing. It's like an arm that's never used; it withers and eventually falls off. I taught my four children to value their sense of knowing, and all four told me that their intuition lessened once they started college, because they had to spend so much time on intellectual pursuits.

I pointed out to one mother that her five-year-old daughter was extremely intuitive and warned against brushing aside things the child said that normally wouldn't fit. They were at the shopping mall one afternoon, and the mother said, "We'd better get home before Daddy gets in." The little girl replied in a matter-of-fact tone, "No, Mommy, Daddy's already home." It was another two hours before he would have normally been home, according to his everyday schedule. As they drove into their driveway, they saw, sure enough, Daddy's car was there.

This same child was sitting on the floor while her mother was listening to the news. As the weather forecaster discussed the hot weather of the season, the little girl said, "Mommy, it's going to snow." About four days later it snowed. The mother told me that had I not said anything to her about her daughter, she would have thought the statement ridiculous, as it had snowed in that area only a couple of times in the past twenty years.

I worked on the case of a young boy who had been abducted and killed. When I first explained to the parents that I felt this child was very intuitive and had tried to express his fear of something he sensed was going to happen, the parents loudly protested that this had never taken place. They did not want to believe that they had ignored anything he said that would have warned of his death.

Following two days discussing this with them, the mother said, "Oh, yes. I remember that for two or three weeks before his disappearance, he started asking if he was going to die." Several nights as she tucked him in bed, he would ask, "Mommy, am I going to die?" She would brush the question aside with reassurance that this was not going to happen.

Now, this was a little boy about seven years old who had never discussed death. It had never been a subject in the house, but it was something he sensed.

Of course, any parent would want to reassure a child that he or she wasn't going to die. But I am constantly telling parents and educators, "Listen to children." If they act differently, ask them what it is. Have them explain why they feel that way. Did they recently hear something on television or at school? Or do they have an intuitive feeling? Did someone say something that is really bothering them?

A similar case was that of a little girl who drowned. She loved to draw pictures of people. The day before she drowned, she began putting bright light, like halos, around the people in her pictures. She said, "I don't know why, Mommy. I can just see lots of bright light around people." Now this little girl loved to draw, and she did it every day, but never before had she done this. Being an only child, she did get a lot of attention from her parents, and the mother took time to ask why her drawings had changed. It caught the mother's attention, but she did not attach any great importance to it, beyond the understanding that something had changed in her daughter's drawing.

The next day the girl went down by the river. Normally the riverbed was so dry that she and the other children played in it. When she went out to play, it was after several days of rain. The river was swollen, full of water rushing near the edge of the banks. She picked up a stick, tried to measure how deep the water was, and fell off the slippery bank into the river. The current washed her away.

I haven't yet worked on a case of a kidnapping, murder, or untimely death of a child where the child hadn't conveyed fear or signaled something to the parents. The children may not know why they feel as they do, but they know it's a feeling of apprehension or fear. It has shown up the same in adults.

A professional couple once came to me. They lived in a home located in one of the secluded valleys of Northern California. They had three children—one was a daughter who had been away at college. As she had driven away from a friend's party one summer, she had misjudged a turn on the narrow country road, causing her to hit a tree and die. While the mother was in my office talking to me, I mentioned that the mother had intuitively sensed the accident ahead of time. "You know," she pondered, "It's really true. Lately it had been coming to me often that we'd been really lucky with our family. Everything had been going so well, it seemed to be too good to be true." After the accident, her husband told her he had experienced the same feeling several times prior to the accident.

They both had been experiencing the feeling of their family being too lucky, but they had never stopped to ask why. From where did the fear emanate? Where did it belong? How could they clarify what they were feeling?

I remember a story about Abraham Lincoln. He had had a vivid dream, and he told a close friend it was troubling him. In the dream, Lincoln saw people weeping in the White House, standing before a coffin. He asked a soldier who had died. The soldier told him the president had been killed by an assassin. A few days later Lincoln was assassinated.

Dreams are often intuition surfacing—feelings that you wouldn't look at during your waking hours. It is a sense of knowing that "seeps in," demanding attention, forcing itself to the surface to be recognized.

Intuition is a sense of knowing *before* you can put words or actions to the situation, and it involves the use of all of your five senses: taste, touch, sound, sight, and smell. In order to reach down and get in touch with your intuitive feeling, you have to relax and put your other senses aside, so that distracting noises, permeating odors, visual movement, anything your taste buds have not adjusted to, restrictive clothing, or body position do not overpower the intuitive sense. It is a means of getting answers, a shortcut to making decisions, and a valuable source of information not otherwise received.

How often have you hung up the telephone and grumbled to yourself, "Why did I even bother with those people? I knew that deal wouldn't go through!" Or you had the feeling it was too good to be true, and it was.

A medical doctor, who valued my advice, called and asked me about a nurse he was thinking of hiring. He had a large office with clientele from all over the world. He told me her name, and I told him, "Well, I think she's a nice, honest, friendly person. But you're not going to get the work out of her you need. She doesn't have the energy level to keep up the pace. I feel like it would be a mistake." Well, he was desperate and needed a nurse, so he hired her.

A couple of months later, he called and said, "Boy, were you ever right! I kept finding her in the back eating jelly sandwiches, cake, and all kinds of sweets. Sometimes she even fell asleep back there. I tested her and found she had low blood sugar, which prevents her from having the energy to get through the day." He wanted to let me know how accurate I had been. He agreed that intuition is a valuable shortcut, if used properly. Many companies have paid me to evaluate people they wanted to hire, products they wanted to put on the market, and partnerships they wanted to form.

All intuitive feelings come to you as a delicate flash. Holding onto and interpreting that flash requires educating your intuition, much the way your intellect and other senses were educated.

Though born with eyes, babies do not know what they see until it is identified for them. The same is true with hearing, touching, tasting, and smelling. How many times did your mother say to you as a child, "This is a dog. The dog goes bow-wow. Where is the cat? The cat goes meow. See the cow. The cow goes moo-moo. And what does a rooster say? Cock-a-doodle-doo!" Your mother educated your sight and hearing the same way she developed your taste. I can remember sitting at the kitchen table with my children, saying, "Eat your potatoes. These are the carrots. Try your carrots. Here's the chocolate pudding. Yum-yum. Isn't that good?"

My daughter loves flowers. As a baby we had to identify each one. How many times have you seen a baby experience the sense of touch by feeling the fur of an animal for the first time? Even today, if one of your five senses experiences something unfamiliar, you must have it identified for future reference.

Maybe you have been in a restaurant and tried a new dish. Perhaps it was something you liked, and you wanted to know its ingredients. Though you have the sense of taste, you couldn't identify this new experience. You had to ask someone to identify it the first time.

Even though you have eyes, the first time you saw a painting, your eyes didn't know what they were seeing. Someone told you it was a painting and perhaps who the artist was.

Through association you became educated to understand things the way most other people do. You have been taught to identify. Intuition was not trained like the other senses, because people cannot see, touch, taste, smell, or hear it. But once you know what it is, you can exercise it and integrate it into a more successful life, because intuition is usually more accurate than the other senses. My reason for saying this is because it's known that a good magician can fool your sight by making you believe that you saw a woman being cut in half or a rabbit being pulled out of a hat. A good con artist can convince your ears that you're hearing about a wonderful deal.

Your other senses can also be fooled. As a child, were you ever at a Halloween party where someone blindfolded you and then passed objects around? You would smell, touch, hear, or taste them, but you weren't sure what they were. You can deceive these senses. The sense of intuition, however, is more difficult to fool if you educate and learn to depend on it.

The first time I met with Dr. Targ and Dr. Puthoff, they said to me, "You know, Kay, for our research program we flew in people from the far reaches of the world who were reported to have a strong sense of intuition. And after a year or two of this, we realized our secretary in the front office could do the same thing." These learned scientists discovered that everyone is intuitive, which is what I've been saying for years. This discovery made a drastic change in their expense account!

If you take intuition and plug it in, you're ahead of people that don't exercise it, because the more you exercise it, the greater you can align with it and utilize it. Think of a television. When you turn it on, it picks up waves another machine is putting out. It receives a program. This type of connection is relevant to people as well. Have you ever walked into a room and immediately known you disliked someone? No one had told you anything about the person, and you had never met before, yet for no apparent reason you disliked him or her. Intuitively you picked up that person's program, which included a dislike for something that was happening in his or her life. You merely reflected it back and believed you disliked that person.

Once, while attending a party at a country club in Carmel, California, I met a man who was suntanned, a picture of vitality and health. He was extremely nice, but after meeting him, I intuitively attempted to avoid any further conversation. I found when this man was near that something made me feel uneasy in his presence. A few days later someone told me what had befallen this same man just a couple of days after the party. He had gone to see his doctor for a physical. At that time it was discovered that he had terminal cancer. I then knew this was the unpleasant feeling that had prevented me from enjoying his company that evening.

It's the same when you meet people you really like. I will guarantee you that they like themselves. They're happy about where they are in the world, and you pick up their feelings—which makes you happy to be with them. It's the same when you watch a television show that makes you laugh and feel good. It actually has nothing to do with you, but it does affect you. We must be in touch with our own programs, and when we notice it change, whether slightly or drastically, we need to take the time to understand it.

When I notice a change in my feelings, I always ask myself, "Who's the matter with me?" not *"What's* the matter with me?" My children have heard me express this so often that they have promised my epitaph will read, She's not really dead, just picking up someone else's condition.

Something important to me is to point out to parents and educators how to recognize intuition in children. Parents have a tendency to brush off children's comments as prattle, because, of course, children are young and haven't been *taught* this feeling. If we listened to children, we would discover that youngsters make very intuitive statements.

I have beaten this drum ever since a head of the National Board of Education once flew out from Washington to discuss with me her role in the future of education. She agreed that people shouldn't bury their children's intuition, that it deserved to be educated along with the mind and body. But so far I've seen no evidence of changes taking place in that area.

During a recent plane trip from Washington, D.C., to San Francisco, I spent an enjoyable time talking with a man who was the president of the board of education in one of the California counties.

He, accompanied by teachers and other members of the board, was returning from a visit with President Reagan at the White House. Their school had received honors as one of the top educational institutes in America. During our conversation this man wholeheartedly agreed that he had reason to believe all children show outward signs of natural intuition. Before we landed, several teachers joined the conversation, agreeing 100 percent that they each had experiential evidence supporting the theory.

How much longer will it be before school systems acknowledge intuition as a valid sense? It's like saying, "You've got eyes, kids, but close them." It never ceases to amaze me that our intuition was present before we developed a vocabulary or perfected our other senses, but it's the last one—if ever—to be educated!

Our intuition senses something in its purest form before our other senses cloud over the knowledge. We may look at it with our eyes and say it doesn't look like that, or have our ears telling us it sounds like something else. Everything in our world is identified with our intuition. If we relied on this pure form of identification, the world would seem very different to us. When combining intuition with intellect, we have an unbeatable combination.

Your intellect is the knowledge and understanding you carry from experience and study. It is the computer in which you store your knowledge, the dictionary that holds your facts and meanings. Thus your intellect translates your intuitive feelings, and, by this process, helps you put those feelings into mental pictures. The translation of your intuition is only as accurate as the degree of your intellect.

A doctor with a higher sense of intuition will make better and faster diagnoses than a doctor who works only from medical journals. Lawyers working with intuition will win more cases in court than those who just apply what they learned in law school. Having worked with many detectives on homicide cases, I know the best ones always use their intuitive feelings. They don't go by "Just the facts, ma'am!"

Intuition combined with little intellect gives you only half the information. I knew a woman who learned at her mother's knee to read tea leaves. She called me when I was in California and said, "Oh, Kay, I see a big white animal around you. It's like a big white bear. Oh, that's bad luck. Big white bears are bad luck." I thought to myself, Oh, come on, now. My intellect tells me I'm not going to the San Francisco Zoo and crawl into a cage with some big white polar bear.

And I'm not planning to trek through Alaska anytime soon. So where is she catching me with a big white bear?

Two or three days later, I was at a cocktail party at a friend's house in Los Angeles. The people throwing the party had a big, white, fluffy Samoyed dog. She was a girl dog, and it was that time of year for her to feel romantic. During the cocktail hour someone let her out of the house by mistake. Later I saw her down the street having a mad love affair with a neighborhood mongrel. Now, it was bad luck for the owners, bad luck for the dog (I guess), but it wasn't bad luck for me. This woman was able to give me her intuitive symbols from looking at the leaves, but she didn't put them together with her intellect.

Intuition is the mortar that holds the facts together. Without the mortar, the bricks of intellect would remain scattered and loosely piled.

Fifteen years ago a young woman taking my course in California struggled to blend her intuition with her intellect. She had already earned two doctorates in different aspects of business and was then studying to become a medical doctor. For the first month of classes, this woman exclaimed, "I just can't feel anything. No matter how hard I try, I can't *feel* anything!" She diligently attended class, took notes like she'd been taught all her life, but couldn't interpret how she felt. During class she sat in the room filing thoughts as they marched into her head, while her feelings quietly waited over in the corner. She had spent so many years in educational institutions—cramming her intellect full of knowledge—that she'd totally forgotten the feeling of intuition. Toward the end of the course, when I was about to give up the hope that she would ever become acquainted with her intuition, she joyously exclaimed, "I felt it! I felt it!"

Think of intuition as a lake. You can sit on the shore, look at it, and never go in, but be aware it's there. You can wade in it or swim to all its depths. I believe intuition is that way. It's there for us to plunge into, but many of us never even get our feet wet.

Do as innocent children do, and trust your intuition. With practice, you will be able to tell the difference between it and imagination or wishful thinking.

THREE

The ABCs of Intuition

In 1936 a television was able to receive signals from a distance of 1 mile. Three years later signals were transmitted 130 miles. With the advancement of knowledge, it is now an everyday occurrence for programs to reach around the world. These programs are sent into the air and broadcast unknown to our five senses, unless we turn on the television to receive a station. If we could physically see these many programs crossing the airwaves, imagine what it would look like if each were a different hue. The sky would be jammed with a tangled mass of streaking colors—it would be one grand laser light show.

BROADCASTING

For purposes of illustration in this section, I'm going to ask you to think of yourself as a television, but always remember that we are more complex and more interesting. People can perform more intricately than any machine ever invented. Therefore, why are we amazed when we find out that we broadcast our own programs? Broadcasting is what we are all constantly doing. It's a proven fact that everything produces an energy field. Your energy field is your program, which consists of who you are and everything you've experienced in life. The important thing to know is that if you could see or hear your own program, then you could easily pick it out from all the others surrounding you. You would then know that all other programs are being sent from someone or something else. Earlier I asked if you had ever walked into a room and immediately disliked someone for no apparent reason. If so, you were intuitively picking up that person's program. If you had stopped to see what you were reacting to, you would have discovered it was something negative in the other person's broadcast. Perhaps that person was unhappy with something in his or her life and you picked up that program and mirrored it back. Or that person was just the sort of person whose program clashed with yours.

Take a look at one woman, who is fighting mad at her husband and joins three of her friends for a game of bridge. While the cards are being shuffled and played, this woman spews out her anger concerning her husband. She spends the next few hours expounding on every husband's failings. As the card game progresses, the other women pick up her broadcast and eventually are in complete accord with her feelings. She sends three other women home ready to divorce their husbands at the first opportune moment. It will take some time before these three wives are once more in touch with their own programs concerning their husbands.

A television broadcast can have the same effect on you. The next time you watch television, whatever is being broadcast is going to affect you when you receive it. If it's a comedy, you will laugh and forget any previous problems. A sad story may bring tears to your eyes; you will be melancholy until you get back to feeling your own program. If it's a good commercial, you might buy that product the next time you go shopping and recommend it to someone else. When you vote for your favorite politicians, question whether you have bought the programs they directed to you or their real programs. These programs may have nothing to do with who you are. They are just being broadcast through the airwaves for anyone to receive.

What amazes me most are the types of programs many people are listening to nowadays. Just stop and think about the millions of people affected by Jim and Tammy Bakker's program. Those two had to be strong broadcasters to have many poor people rush out and mail them their last dollar, convinced this was what they wanted to do.

Thousands of people reacted to the Bakkers' program, which was what the Bakkers wanted. Look at the response to Ollie North! He could have shredded the Declaration of Independence and convinced some people, with his broadcast of concern and dedication, that it was the right thing to do. Many people are still carrying his program like a banner.

If the program being broadcast is strong enough, it can overwhelm people who are not in touch with their own. Look at what Jim Jones did with his People's Temple. How could hundreds of people so willingly play out his program and drink Kool-Aid laced with poison and obediently lie down and die?

Another well-known program came from an ex-taxi driver who left his wife and children, changed his name, and moved to the West Coast to become a multimillionaire. How could he do this unless his program was so intense that thousands of people jumped at the chance to spend several hundred dollars for his course, during which he referred to them as assholes and denied them access to the bathroom.

Some famous people who have influenced their countries or the entire world with the programs they broadcast: Gandhi, Mother Theresa, Adolf Hitler, Joan of Arc, Rasputin, Martin Luther King, Jr., and Eva Perón.

If a single program can be strong enough to influence a large number of people, a family or neighborhood program can be even stronger, and a city or national broadcast can be unbelievably powerful. If these programs are in unison, then what they are broadcasting is intensified immensely.

I mention in my first book the heavy, oppressive feeling of Belfast. It's a place where war has gone on for so long, the same program has been played so long, that the people don't even really remember why they began fighting. A Belfast psychiatrist once told me, "If the war stopped today, every person in Belfast would need psychiatric care." This is because once the long-running program stopped, the people would not know how to switch their broadcast from hate and animosity to love and understanding toward the so-called other side.

Inanimate as well as animate objects broadcast programs. A stock will give off a program if you take the time to examine it intuitively. You can place it on an imaginary graph and see how high or low it goes; then you will know where it has been in the past, where it is in the present, and what the future holds for that stock. Understanding the ABCs will also enable you to read different broadcasts, perhaps the broadcast of someone you contemplate going into business with, a person applying for a job, or a particular product you might market.

When I'm asked to check a particular person for business partnership, I look to see if the people are compatible, if their personal lives will cause problems at work, if their health is strong enough, and if one of them will have to do all the work. I have a list that needs to be checked off in each program to see if certain people will be compatible. I've also worked for a number of large corporations screening prospective executives by using my checklist. Besides telling the corporation which people were best for the job, I found myself at times telling the person applying for the position that it wasn't the right job for him or her. After explaining the reasons, the person would admit it really wasn't what he or she wanted to be doing. All this information comes from the other person's program. If you listen to your intuition, it will be an important source of information and save you a lot of steps and possible mistakes.

Some mistakes I've seen or made while under the influence of a strong program are the suicide of one person for another person's depression, surgery for someone else's pain, the taking of aspirin for a friend's headache, and assent to someone else's program. I've even heard of extremes, such as a tribe in Australia that scientists have studied. When somebody from the tribe commits a crime, the village leader sends out a broadcast strong enough to kill the culprit. The leader, without uttering a word, points a bone in that person's direction with an accompanying broadcast for him or her to drop dead. Even though the person may be out of sight and running through the bush, he or she obliges the leader and dies. When found, scientists are unable to find any sign of physical harm to these people's bodies, other than the fact that their hearts have stopped.

Space has nothing to do with how well you interpret or send a program. You can learn to receive or broadcast from Washington to Moscow as easily as you can to someone across the room.

People often ask how I can intuit a program coming from the past or future, as well as one taking place at the moment. With my intuition I'm able to reach into the past, present, and future because all programs are part of a continuous, unseen hemisphere. The only reason time seems to be separated is because it's measured in space, as in hours, weeks, months, years. We created the clock and gave it dividing markers to organize life for more convenience. Therefore time is not naturally defined or separated. (I personally dislike having a clock dictate my life. If we let our intuitive feelings be our clock, we would always be at the right place at the right time and stay for the right duration. Of course, that's why many of my friends send me social invitations with my arrival time set for two hours prior to the rest of the guests. They have hopes that I might at least arrive with everyone else. Their hopes are usually dashed.)

Eastern thought teaches time as something cyclical, continuing again and again to infinity. Western thought conceives time as something linear, having a beginning, middle, and end. Let me create an example of time for you by using a river. As you sit on the bank of the Amazon River, you can see part of the flowing river; green, leafy trees; and several vines. That part of the river is the present. But an astronaut's view while in space is of the Amazon in its entirety as it winds through the jungle. From an objective point of view you can see the beginning of the river, which is the past; around the bends and through the middle, which is the present; and where it enters the ocean, which is the future.

A San Francisco attorney called me concerning his niece, who was missing. She'd been vacationing in Hawaii with her family and had never returned following her morning jog. Her uncle requested the Hawaiian detective to phone me in California. As I scanned her program, I told the detective he would find her just before reaching the other end of the path her family had said she normally jogged each morning. What I did was pick up the woman's program at the time she left her room—how she felt, what she thought—and interpret her feelings as she jogged away from the hotel. By following her program, I was able to check to see if she was afraid. Was someone following her? Had she been threatened? Before she reached the end of the path, I watched her being pulled off the path, out of sight, into thick, tropical foliage, where the altercation took place. I intuitively searched the scene and found she was missing one tennis shoe and was no longer able to move. That's when I picked up the program of the assailant, the physical appearance of the assailant, and other descriptive information for the detective. This was done over a twenty-four-hundred-mile distance. Just as an astronaut has an objective view of the river, I could visualize as she moved from the past, into the present, and into her future, which led to her death.

If the president asked me to monitor the head of Russia's armed forces, it would be totally possible. As we've discussed, space would not be an issue. Days or months might pass that I wouldn't sense anything unusual going on in this man's life other than too much vodka one night, a heated disagreement with his wife, or a meeting in which he struggled to make his point clear in a room of officials. Then suddenly one day I might feel that something of importance to America was about to happen. At that point I would pick up the details concerning the country in question, such as the type of people who lived in that country, the language spoken, the impact any decision made about this country would have on America. The experts could then take these facts and draw many conclusions. This method is much like the way I work with detectives.

When working with law enforcement officers, I give them as many facts as possible about the missing person's location; I describe the surrounding physical area, mentioning, for example, if it includes trees, a desert, or a house. Once they have the facts, they can begin to match them with their knowledge of their part of the country. It's as if I describe a piece of a puzzle to them and they find out where it fits. Intuition can be used for highly precise work.

Because other programs flow and ebb around us, they constantly create an atmosphere that affects us in minor and major ways. When you choose a restaurant for dinner, why do you prefer that restaurant to another? Is it the food and decor or the programs broadcast by the owner and employees? Both have an effect on you. The comfort of your chair and the colors that surround you can make a difference in your dining enjoyment. So if you've had a hectic day, don't select a restaurant with reds, yellows, and oranges, because they will not allow you to relax but create the feeling that you must rush through your meal and leave. If the maître d' has been accommodating and the people have served you graciously, you will feel the difference between this and a restaurant of irritating programs. When the chef puts love and care into the preparation of the food, it's more likely to agree with your digestive system. These are the reasons why you place a restaurant on the list of your favorites.

Have you ever gone into a place to have your car fixed or buy a product and found you wanted to leave immediately? It's the same thing. A merchant's program, if unpleasant, can have such a profound effect on you that you never return.

If you own a business, you should realize the broadcast you are sending out can make a difference in how large a clientele you attract. If happy people work for you, customers will sense their pleasant program, causing your business to become more successful.

The ABCs
of Intuition

I wonder why entrepreneurs and professionals seldom consider the effect the program they emanate has on prospective clients. Surely you have patronized a company that created such a strong reaction in you that you selected another place of business. It happened to me recently while I was in a new dentist's office. As he examined my teeth, I knew I would never go back to him. It had nothing to do with his ability or the work he performed that day, just the fact that I didn't feel comfortable in his office. Others less sensitive than I am will also find themselves making a change without realizing why they did it. Try to get in touch with the feelings you have about your doctor, dentist, attorney, hairstylist, butcher, baker, and others providing you with a service. Do you feel like taking your business elsewhere, and why?

An orthodontist in California is so aware of the importance of the feelings his staff give to patients in his office that he had me devise a course for his dentists, dental assistants, and receptionists. He understands how their programs can affect the patient and vice versa. After consulting with me he decided to have a room designed where each member of his staff could go through the color exercise. (We will discuss this in detail in Chapter Six.) This enables them to relinquish all programs before and after a day's work. His several offices have thrived beyond belief, because of his understanding of the importance of everything that can affect a person's six senses. Nothing was left to chance, including the color of each room and piece of furniture.

If you knew the intuitive sense could make you a pauper or millionaire, wouldn't you include that information in your business plan?

RECEIVING

Besides broadcasting our own programs, we receive programs from others in varying degrees. Unlike the television you watch at home, you have a limitless range of reception. You are intuitively receiving different programs every minute of every day on one of three levels: low, medium, or high. Every living thing has an intuitive sense, though the level of reception may differ. This is an inborn part of you, and with daily practice, you can receive a broadcast from anyone or anything, anywhere. Consider, for example, how many accounts you have heard of an animal finding its way over hundreds of miles of strange terrain to locate an owner who had moved. The pet was merely tuning in to and tracking the owner's program.

Let's investigate the various ways that each of us receive. People with a higher level of reception are often referred to as sensitive, perceptive, or intuitive. However you refer to it, it all means the same thing. They're similar to those who have an affinity for sports because of better muscle coordination. Except for those with a physical handicap, we can all learn to throw a baseball—but not everyone can make the big league. Certain people have an affinity for music because of better hearing or dexterity in their hands. We can all learn how to play the musical scale, but we can't all become noted concert pianists.

Are you someone who feels you must take everything logically, step by step? If so, you'll have to work harder to bring your intuition into play, because logic is strictly using your brain. But don't worry, you can do it, and once you have the other half of the picture, your logic will help you make a checklist to interpret the intuitive feeling.

Low Receivers

We call low receivers insensitive. We've all known people like this. They register few incoming programs. It's the person you've dated for three years, whom you've told again and again not to show up late without calling, but he or she does it anyway. Generally, these people don't pick up programs and cannot understand people's feelings, perhaps not even their own. A low receiver can hear your words again and again but not sense the feeling that accompanies them. It's like having the television on audio but not video. They receive only the words, never the entire picture.

There are reasons for the low receiver to be out of touch. That person may have been born with a defect in his or her makeup. Something physical, emotional, or mental doesn't function properly. It's as if the tubes of the television are blown, so no picture appears. This makes for an imbalance, not allowing the intuition to receive and translate information. Low receivers could have been born into a family that always fought or a family that never allowed anyone to show emotions without ridicule. These programs hurt so much that they shut down to avoid the pain they felt coming from those around them.

These people have learned to disconnect from their feelings. If they are willing to get back in touch with those feelings, however, they can bring their reception up to a higher level.

Medium Receivers

Medium receivers are people I describe as receiving local stations, familiar stations they understand, such as mother, father, spouse, child, long-time friend, or old working associate. They feel comfortable with the same station and tune in to the same newscaster whenever they want information. They're the couple that has been married for years. When the husband walks into the room with a problem, the wife asks, "What's wrong honey?" without even looking up from her knitting.

It's not unusual for the medium receiver to get a feeling about Mother. The feeling gets stronger as the day goes by, so she calls, and, sure enough, Mother's ill. Or the child who knows before getting home that he's going to get into trouble for being late. Even though for six previous days he felt perfectly free about stopping off at Johnny's house and being late, this day he senses something. If a friend you've known for years calls and says, "Hello," you may feel immediately that something's wrong. Medium receivers have gotten to know pretty much what a familiar person feels like, and the minute that program switches, they know something has caused a change in the broadcast. It's like hearing a familiar song with a word or note changed; you recognize that it's somehow different.

The medium receiver could be in a room with twenty televisions broadcasting, but his or her own program would be playing loudest. The person may have learned to regulate the volume so the television always has a medium setting, so that other programs playing else-where aren't disturbing unless they have changed and are no longer familiar. That's when a medium receiver stops and suddenly thinks about Mother, feeling an urge to call because of a nagging hunch that something is wrong. With practice, the medium receiver can increase his or her reception to high.

High Receivers

High receivers must always begin and end the day with their own programs. These people have dials that receive everyone at the same volume—high! Their reception must be handled in a careful way, because it can cause great confusion. This is a person who can have a nervous breakdown, a person whose emotional makeup is very sensitive. High receivers have been known to commit suicide because of someone else's depression. I had a case of a man in college who assisted in committing a robbery. He was from a fine family, didn't need the money, and had never before gotten in trouble. During school he had been spending time with a student who had no respect for the law. Soon he picked up that person's program and believed he wanted to go along with him during a robbery. It was totally against his nature and caused a state of shock when he realized what he had done. This is how respectable, decent people can end up as part of a lynch mob. When one person's feelings are very strong, they can cause a group to act in a way that would normally horrify them.

High receivers will do things they're totally against because they are so sensitive to other people's programs. They can pick up a program just that easily, often without realizing it. That's why these people must work harder to know their own programs, to differentiate them from all the others, because they are constantly being bombarded with others. If they were sitting in a room with twenty televisions broadcasting, they would receive all programs at the same volume. They can be brainwashed by another program if they forget which is their own station. People have to be responsible for their own programs.

For the high receiver it's a matter of staying in touch with who you are and translating which program is affecting you. Make it a point to use my favorite phrase, *"Who's* the matter with me?"* not *"What's* the matter with me?"*

It doesn't hurt for the high receiver to play someone else's program if it helps him or her to understand that person better. Being objective and describing that person's program can help provide a better understanding to both of them. But the high receiver needs to keep in touch with what his or her own program is saying. One way I suggest is for high receivers to start the day by relaxing in the shower and asking themselves how they feel about their family, friends, job, health, finances. They have to bring those intuitive feelings up, take each one and see how it really feels to them. Is it a comfortable feeling? Is it uncomfortable? Is it a happy feeling? A confident feeling? How does each one feel? Like good cooks tasting a recipe, they sort out the different ingredients.

When my daughter was first in college, I had been busy helping build the Teen Club on the naval base in Mayfort, Florida. I was also staging the Miss Duval County Pageant, doing a radio show five days a week, and teaching at my modeling school. My husband was at sea, so I had to be both mother and father. I had not stopped to look at my daughter every day, until one evening we were relaxing over dinner. All of a sudden I realized she was having a problem in school. She had never said a word to me about it, but I knew she was having problems with a professor. When asked, she said, "Yes." It was an art teacher who wanted to make Cindy into a clone of herself, not allowing her to express originality. In my busy schedule I had not taken the time to feel her program to see if there was something I could do to help her. We often pick up feelings from our family without taking the time to define them.

Look at the doctor, or anyone who works intuitively with other people all day. This person will literally feel problems reflected by each person he or she comes into contact with during the day. This is why there is such a high percentage of burnout among psychiatrists, detectives, and other people working in emotionally related fields. This person must learn to disengage from all of the other programs and turn the television down so he or she can hear his or her own program more clearly.

After a day of counseling, I must do the same thing. It often takes a couple of hours before I get back in touch with my program 100 percent. At parties people are always asking, "What's your intuitive feeling about me?" This is like asking a doctor at the same function, "How's my gallbladder?" The doctor's not on call, and neither am I. So I explain, "I've turned off my receiver tonight. After sharing other people's programs all day, I just want to relish how I feel about the party."

Recently a woman was on television with her psychiatrist. The psychiatrist said the woman had several different personalities. They went on to describe them, but I really believe this woman has her volume knob turned up too high. She picks up all these different stations in the air and describes these personalities as her own. They may be coming from many parts of her river, producing information from past, present, and future programs.

It's the same if you meet a friend for lunch and he's extremely depressed. You're going to leave that person, go back to the office, and feel life is not so wonderful after all. It will take you a while to get back to your normal cheerful self, unless you know how to identify that program and the effect it has on you.

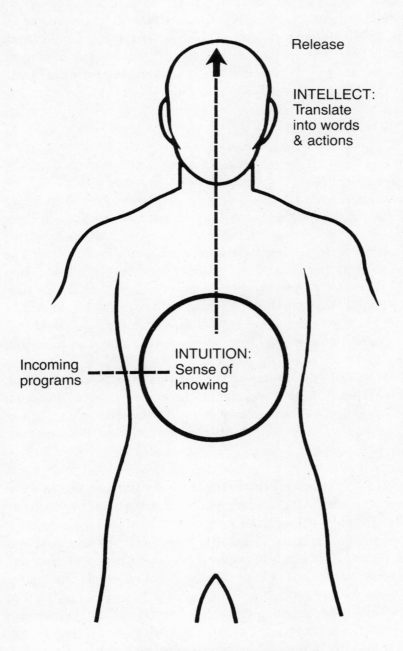

Release

INTELLECT:
Translate
into words
& actions

Incoming
programs

INTUITION:
Sense of
knowing

BASIC INTUITIVE
PROCEDURE

High receivers often ask me to please tell them how to turn their reception *off.* But that's neither possible nor, I believe, desirable. If you turn off your reception, you not only turn off the program that is bothering you, but your ability to receive any program. In other words, *total silence*! What high receivers need to do is learn how to turn the volume *down,* so that others' programs are not blaring at them.

TRANSLATING

An incoming program gives a distinct feeling, which is a message. You always feel it in the pit of your stomach. Normally when someone says, "It makes me feel uneasy," he or she will be holding the stomach while talking, which is the location of the intuitive feeling, "the gut feeling."

The first step to finding your intuition is relaxing the other five senses enough so that you are not aware of anything moving around you, your son's stereo blasting upstairs, any smells in the area, or your clothes being a little too tight because of overindulging at lunch. When you're relaxed enough to get in touch with that special feeling, bring it up and put it with your intellect so it can be translated into meaning.

Dr. Jonas Salk, discoverer of the polio vaccine, once remarked, "It is with excitement that I wake up in the morning wondering what my intuition will toss up to me, like gifts from the sea. I work with it, and rely upon it. It's my partner." (Eugene Raudsepp, "Playing Your Hunches," *San Francisco Chronicle,* 13 Oct. 1982).

After twenty years in this field, I have every reason to feel that our intuitive responses are stimulated by the adrenal glands. The message is sent out with the adrenaline and then received by the brain. The fleeting message is so sudden it can pass untranslated, unless you take the time to focus on it and break it down. First you have the feeling, but let's say you don't know what it means. Ask yourself some questions, such as, If I were going to ask this feeling what it was, what would it tell me? Is it a feeling in my life, or someone else's? If it's a feeling from someone else, what effect does it have on my life? Take that feeling apart with your intellect and describe it aloud or write it down. That way you will hear or see it and know whether you have accurately described what it means. By the time you stop to think about writing and find a pencil, you may have forgotten the feeling, so it might be easier to put it on a cassette tape. Use whatever works best for you, because this delicate flash is not like the chair you sit in, which doesn't move away from you. But you can train yourself to hold onto this feeling for any length of time. Believe me, once the adrenals carry it to your brain, you can hold onto it as long as necessary so that you can look at every aspect.

You'll be amazed at how many variations of the same feeling you can register. Take the feeling of success. How many variations are there? Feelings of success in a minor way. Feelings of success on a project or deal you just closed. Or feelings of this is going to lead me to absolute success in my life. These feelings are just like musical notes that sound a little different but are located next to each other on the same scale. Thus the importance of describing the total feeling aloud or writing it down. When I hear my own words, I often keep searching until I have located the exact word to describe the feeling, adjusting it until I am satisfied.

Your intuition can always be brought up to your intellect, but the translation of that feeling will be only as sophisticated as you are. Your intellect will translate as far as your experiences in life have educated you. If you've touched velvet, you know how it feels. If you've seen and smelled a rose, you know what feeling it gives you. The more times you've experienced something, the more accurately you can translate the feeling associated with it. Take the color red. I say red feels vibrant, energetic, vital to me. But in one class I taught, a psychologist said that red made her feel depressed. There I was expecting her to feel vibrant and excited when I showed the red card, but instead she felt heavy! At that moment it became clear to me that everyone builds his or her own vocabulary to translate intuitive messages.

Let's take cats for another example. If I were to pick up a feeling about a cat, it would be a pleasant one, as I've always felt a home needed a couple of cats to make it warm. But I know people hate cats because they were scratched as children. They would register hate instead of the warmth I feel. If you have a particular feeling about a project coming up, make yourself a checklist that covers all its dimensions. What does it feel like? It's not enough just to say it feels good or bad, so let's break it down. Listed here are a few of the questions you might ask yourself. Take each question, don't rush, and be aware of how it feels. Stay with it until you can describe the feeling completely, then move on to the next one.

1. What's the person you're doing business with feel like? Honest? Dishonest? Energetic? Lazy?

2. Are you going to make enough money on the project?

3. Is the contract going to be signed and become a successful project? Is there something missing in the contract? Have you overlooked anything?

4. If a product's involved, how does it feel? Is it the right time to put it on the market? Is it going to be popular? Should it be changed in any way?

A commercial realtor in one of my courses asked, "How am I going to tell if I'm really going to sell this property or if it's just my wishful thinking?" So I taught her to make a checklist and remain objective about it. She had to mentally drive by the building a month after the the time she began trying to sell it. Once there, she had to look for any changes in the property. Had any of the signs changed? Was there still a For Sale sign on the property? Were there any structural changes, such as new company signs, fresh paint, or different landscaping? If there were, she had to ask the potential customers whether they would change anything, to see if these changes matched what she intuitively felt would happen to that building. She could also intuitively look at the contract when it was being signed. She could intuit what kind of hand was signing it. A man's or woman's? Fair, medium, or dark skin? Then she could check to match it with the hand of anyone who was looking at the property. If you are dealing with an issue that affects you personally, you must have a detailed checklist and translate the feeling thoroughly to be sure wishful thinking is not at work. You have to look at the issue objectively and understand which program you're picking up.

In the beginning, receiving and translating may take you half an hour or so, because you have to consciously relax and get in touch with the feeling. As you exercise your intuition, you will eventually find you can pick up and translate intuitive feelings in a matter of seconds.

Don't be afraid to bring in your other senses when working with your intuition. At first I thought intuition was separate from those senses, but it's not. Once you've gotten in touch with the feeling, it can be combined to work with the other five senses. I work with homicide detectives, and they need many details. They take me beyond just giving a mental picture. I can feel the kind of soil in a given area as if I had picked it up and held it in my hands. Or if they ask me what kind of fabric a person was wearing, I can touch it with my sense of touch and tell them whether it is rough, smooth, or soft. Then I can actually listen for voices and translate how they sound: guttural, southern, northern, or foreign. Or I can hear sounds in the background, such as children playing, water rushing, or city traffic. And my sense of smell translates any unusual odors. In one case I kept telling the detective about an acrid smell. When he got to the area, the first thing he smelled was excess gas that was being burned off nearby gas wells.

Some of the detectives noticed that after a trip to the ladies room I often came out saying, "I just found out something else about the case." It's become a standing joke among the detectives who know me well. If we get hung up on some detail of the case, they say, "Kay. Stop and go to the ladies room, please," because there I can relax and more information will surface. They have also found that if they take me to dinner after a few hours working the case, I relax over my martini and more details pour forth. Their secretaries are always typing information from notes a detective has written on a place mat from a restaurant.

FOUR

Increased Reception

When I used to read Eastern philosophy and its cautioning of the dangers of increasing the energy flow of the seven chakras, I couldn't understand why they warned against stimulating these glands. I thought it ludicrous until I realized that when you increase your energy flow, you increase your reception. And if you increase your reception without being aware of it, you're bound to experience overloading.

I don't believe it's harmful to stimulate the glands as long as you are aware of the increase and understand the potential complications. But constant overstimulation of the adrenals can cause problems. It can become very confusing when the adrenals are stimulated to the point where you cannot translate any program, even your own. It would be the same as plugging your television into a socket of higher voltage. The set shorts out and you have no picture.

Do not increase your reception unless you are ready to translate faster and be more attuned to it. The following are factors that contribute to revving up the adrenals. Believe me, you don't want to stimulate them to the point where you are no longer peacefully driving along the country road at 40 miles per hour but racing into deadman's curve at 120 without realizing it.

The following ways of increasing receptivity are methods that you may have already used, never dreaming that they did increase your intuitive reactions to life.

ALCOHOL

When someone has a couple of drinks, people usually say, "That's his real self coming out." That's not his real self. It's a reaction to half a dozen programs from other people in the room that are merged together, like six television programs being simultaneously broadcast in the same place.

One of my clients found that every time she had a few drinks she would change from a seemingly happy wife to an angry one. When she wasn't drinking she continually convinced herself that she could accept the faults she found in her husband. She carried out daily life holding her tongue about the lack of attention he gave their children. He allowed them to come and go as they pleased, play their stereo at any volume, and watch television when they didn't feel like doing homework. She felt the children needed structure. Besides that, she thought he was an inconsiderate lover.

These things she covered over when not drinking, in order to keep them together. But when she drank, his programs were broadcast stronger and at a louder volume to her. She couldn't not react to them. With the alcohol revving up her intuition, she couldn't tolerate his program. Her reactions came spilling out in the form of anger.

When I was a novice at understanding all this, I learned the hard way with alcohol. At a party one night I looked at a man and asked, "Who was that blonde you gave your key to today?" As he looked at me, startled, a woman approached him from behind, asking, "What key? What blonde?" Realizing I'd picked up his program, I left the poor guy as he was trying to explain to his wife that the blonde was his secretary and he'd given her the key to his office. At least that was his story.

Some of us have a few drinks to relax after a long, hard day. But we always have to remember, those cocktails are going to make us more receptive, and sometimes open us up to places we would rather not, or perhaps should not, be.

DRUGS

When I realized that drugs could distort and pick up so many programs that one person could commit suicide for another person's depression, I became very concerned. I've seen suicide cases where alcohol or drugs were involved and high receivers were unaware of what they were doing. They had picked up so many programs that they couldn't deal with the confusion. The distortion would be comparable to watching a video on fast forward and turning the volume up all the way.

An FBI agent introduced me to the wife of a reputable surgeon who had called the FBI about an unsolved case. While watching the news she had had several flashes of intuition and felt she knew who committed the crime. She called the FBI and said, "I know who did that." They were happy to have any assistance solving a case that was lacking in clues. By the time an agent got to her, however, she had forgotten the feeling and the information. After the initial impact, she couldn't hold onto the feeling, take it apart, and put it together with her intellect.

The agent, who had previously worked with me, called to ask if I would be able to assist her in pulling out information they could use. Upon meeting with the woman, I decided to look her program over and find out why this was suddenly happening to her—why she was a medium receiver who had suddenly shifted to high and didn't know how to cope with it. I finally realized the culprit was the three different bouts of surgery she had had in the past year. The stress of each surgery, plus the necessary drugs, had stimulated her adrenal glands, which had increased her intuition to the point of receiving bits and pieces of ongoing programs. But the woman couldn't translate the information. Not understanding the circumstances, she was completely confused from picking up snatches of unfamiliar programs, and she worried that perhaps she was losing her mind.

After the counseling, I asked if she wanted to remain as a high receiver or return to her normal level of reception. She preferred to go back to where she was more comfortable. So I explained how she could calm down the adrenals, which would regulate the intuitive flashes.

After working on hundreds of homicide cases, I did some research on the rate of drug-related homicides and murders prior to the coming of the drug age (the 1960s), compared with that period and the period following. The increase of drug-related cases was frightening. While working on the numerous cases where persons committing crimes were on drugs, I found that they appeared totally disconnected from any feeling of responsibility concerning their actions. There were no signs of remorse or regret for their crimes, which ranged from robbery to sadistic murder. I have recently heard that the homicide rate of Washington, D.C., is something like 85 percent drug-related. This is devastating.

If we stopped and looked at the statistics of what drugs are doing to our culture, we would be amazed. Each of us must learn to accept responsibility for our own program, the tremendous effect our program has on others, and the complications that arise when we increase our intuitive reception.

During my years studying the effect intuition has on our physical, emotional, and mental processes, I was fortunate to meet a medical doctor who had studied this. Dr. Yiwen Tang of Reno, Nevada, had graduated from Harvard Medical School and was practicing preventive medicine when I met him in San Francisco. He explained that he had changed from internal to preventive medicine because he had not been satisfied with the rate of patient cure.

Preventive medicine includes the study of all aspects of the body's chemistry and what the results are if the body lacks or produces the wrong levels of chemicals. A piece of information Dr. Tang shared with me was simple yet profound. A body whose chemistry is normal will always renew itself. A body whose chemistry is out of balance will eventually develop diseases. This I have seen happen over and over again in my clients. The different stresses, excesses, and suppressions I mention in the following sections are some of the ways your body chemistry can be thrown off.

DIET

Caffeine, sugar, and chocolate increase adrenal flow. They are the false stimulants most of us reach for when needing a lift. They make the body machinery run faster. Any time more stress is added to a certain part of an engine, the engine is more likely to break down. It's the same when we overstress the adrenals, and incoming information can't reach the rest of the body so that it can compensate to handle it. Eventually, you have emotional, physical, or mental stress.

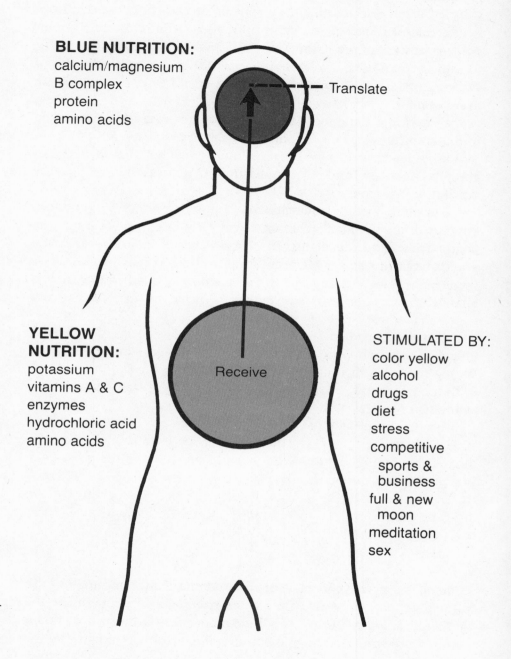

BLUE NUTRITION:
calcium/magnesium
B complex
protein
amino acids

Translate

YELLOW NUTRITION:
potassium
vitamins A & C
enzymes
hydrochloric acid
amino acids

Receive

STIMULATED BY:
color yellow
alcohol
drugs
diet
stress
competitive
  sports &
  business
full & new
  moon
meditation
sex

Vegetarians must learn to combine the right foods to supply the body with enough protein. It's important to do this because protein is necessary for healthy and stabilized adrenal flow, which helps you better monitor incoming programs by keeping the volume adjusted as needed. You want to receive just one program at a time and identify it, instead of several programs charging in together and thus being untranslatable. Protein keeps the adrenals from being too stimulated. It slows the transmission down so you can manage an incoming feeling and translate it before receiving another one.

If you're trying to bring intuition up and combine it with the intellect, it's important that you have the right nutrients. If you are lacking in protein foods, which often also include the B-complex vitamins, amino acids, and minerals such as calcium, then you'll find that you're receiving many programs but making no intellectual translation. You need fruits and vegetables for sensitivity, but that's where your focus will stay unless you have the protein to draw your focus up to the brain. It's important to understand how the merger of intuition and intellect work, but just as important to understand how to eat so that the merger can happen. If you find yourself being very sensitive but unable to translate, I recommend you visit your doctor or a good nutritionist to find out what's lacking in your diet.

STRESS

Stress can also make you think and react quickly. When I was expecting my third child in a matter of days, I remarked to my husband that the car brakes didn't seem to be working well. As I dropped him off at his squadron on the naval base, I mentioned it again. His response was, "Oh, that's all right, honey. Don't worry about it."

Being Catholic, I was in the habit of saying a quick little prayer to St. Christopher before embarking on a long trip. This time, to my surprise, I found myself saying, "St. Christopher, be my guide," prior to the short trip across town to my doctor's office.

While driving down a hill toward an intersection that had four lanes of traffic crossing it, the light turned red. I pressed on the brakes, but the car kept moving on down the hill. In that instant I looked in every direction, managed to turn with the flow of crossing traffic, and stayed as close to the curb as I could. Fortunately, an elderly woman was able to move into the next lane, but not before she saw her life pass before her eyes. I grabbed the emergency brake just before I would have hit a parked car, and then sat there wondering how I had done all that in a matter of seconds. I reached down, patted my tummy, and said to the child within, "Your name is Christopher. Or, if you're a girl, it's Christine." As it turned out, the baby became Christopher. I've often wondered if St. Christopher stayed with me in the car while I went around that wild turn, or if he sat on the curb and cheered me on.

Have you ever been in an emergency situation where, without consciously realizing it, you worked everything out? The stress of the moment increased your adrenal flow, which increased your reception. Then you translated and reacted accordingly.

Stress on the adrenals can affect all areas—physical, emotional, and mental. And if you burn out one area, it will cause problems in other areas, because they have to work harder to compensate.

SEX

I usually throw in the subject of sex at the end of my lectures to see if everyone's listening. Homicide detectives always perk up at that point, wondering what I'm going to teach them new about sex. It's not really anything new, unless you didn't realize that sex increases your intuition because your adrenals are stimulated. Haven't you felt more attuned to your partner after sex? Maybe you don't feel that way a day or two afterward, but you do during the sensuous night. If ever two people are attuned to each other, it is at that moment of sharing intense feelings. One word of caution—never let your passion disguise the intuitive input of the moment.

COMPETITION

Competitive sports and competition in work stir up your adrenaline, which again encourages intuitive flashes. The stimulation will be as vigorous as the situation and will slow down again afterward. The increase can be beneficial if you need to get something up and out of your system, but it's not always advantageous.

The blue man, the mental type, can look at a football game objectively during his physical participation. He uses his mind to plan strategy, know when to apply strength effectively, and know how to recognize a team's weakness. Should he lose the game, his mind rationalizes the facts and circumstances in a way that allows him to accept the defeat. His life continues unshattered by one loss.

The physical reactor, the red man, goes into the game with all his physical machinery at fever pitch and plays to the fullest. His physical reactions happen without him laboring in thought. After winning or losing the game, he drops with satisfaction, because he has had a good workout. If he had a defeat, he kicks a few lockers before feeling complete.

The intuitive man, yellow, whose adrenals are stimulated not only by exercise but also by his sensitivity, has a slightly different program. He feels the excitement of the event, but can also pick up feelings and thoughts of defeat that the other team is projecting his way. He may be as intelligent as the blue, as magnificently physical as the red, but he works from his intuition. He responds to the stress with overstimulation of the adrenals. One result can be that when the line of opposition runs toward him, he can sense their rushing thoughts of "Crush, kill, destroy!" causing him to be on his toes. Or he may pick up on which way the other team is planning to execute its next move. Watch the top-notch athletes. They always seem to be in the right place at the right time. It's because they intuitively pick up the other team's program and plan. It's the same for people in marketing, sales, or any area of competition.

My husband's squadron used to compete with other squadrons in a bombing derby. They would go out for a week and compete against each other to see who hit the most targets and had the best timing. It was the most intuitive pilots who really zeroed in on the targets. A Navy pilot who makes a living taking off from an aircraft carrier in the middle of an ocean has, or soon develops, a keen intuition. His life depends on sensing the position of the plane, the ship, and himself. I found this sharp intuition in Navy pilots, as well as in homicide detectives. A strong urge for survival sharpens the sense of intuition.

Perhaps you have watched cats as they leap from one spot to another. You will notice that they stop and really intuit the place where they are going to land. You can actually see them take their time, get in touch with the feeling, and follow through with the jump.

Increased
Reception

THE MOON

Doctors have discovered that both the full moon and the new moon create more extreme responses in people: more bleeding, more pain, and more irrational actions. Emergency room personnel and police officers can tell you stories about the increase in traumatic incidents at these times.

Just think about it. The moon controls the tides. The highest content by weight in the human body is water, so don't you think the moon will affect you?

The drapes in my bedroom are lined with blackout lining, but believe me, I can tell a full moon. On a night when I lie in bed with my eyes wide open and don't know why, because I haven't paid attention to the moon's waxing and waning, I realize (around 4:00 A.M.) that there's a full moon outside.

RELAXING

Relaxation increases your intuitive awareness. If your body is uptight, the mind overpowers any ability to get in touch with your feelings. If you're tired or stressed, it's much harder to get in touch with your intuition.

So what is relaxation really? It is not using any one sense to an extreme. You're not focused on a loud noise outside, an odd taste in your mouth, a strange smell, a movement within the range of your vision, the tightness of your clothes or shoes—none of the senses is focused on anything in particular. When you reach that level, you can sit down and have a chat with your intuition.

When you relax and dim your other senses, allowing the intuitive sense to flow through you, you must recognize that you are then a receiver of programs. You need to carefully interpret whose programs they are and how they affect you. I say this because several clients have come to me because of problems following the completion of a self-awareness or relaxation course. One problem with these courses is that they may offer little understanding of what can take place when you increase your level of sensitivity. You cannot increase your awareness of your program without increasing your awareness of other programs. If you're more aware of yourself, you're more aware of everything in the universe.

Early one morning I received a telephone call from a woman who was obviously in a state of turmoil. She stated that she had been referred to me and desperately needed an appointment. When I looked at my appointment book, nothing was available for the next two months, so I attempted to allay her fears until I could see her. When I asked if she would relate her problem to me, she replied with a voice filled with acute embarrassment. She was a single woman in her middle years, raised in a conservative and reserved southern family. It took time to gently pry the story from her, because she had great difficulty speaking of intimate details.

The previous month she had enrolled in a mind control course in hopes of increasing her awareness. "In the course we're taught to lie down on our bed, relax, and get in touch with all of our feelings just before we go to sleep. After several weeks of this, I'm experiencing ..." There was a long, uncomfortable pause. "Emotions of a sexual nature." She had approached her instructor and asked if there was anything in the course that could be causing this to take place. The instructor had indignantly told her not to be foolish, flatly refusing to take any responsibility for her newly awakened feelings.

I explained to her that turning up her volume, increasing reception, meant she would become more aware not only of herself but also of everything that surrounded her. And being single, her sexuality had always been under control, causing this to be extremely frightening for her. The poor woman felt like she was about to lose her mind, because the person teaching the course was totally unaware that this kind of exercise would cause her to become more sensitive on all levels—physical, emotional, and mental.

The next question was, Why would she absorb more stimuli on the physical level than on the other two? I asked her to give me details about the room where she practiced the exercise. She described the bedspread, drapes, and chaise lounge as being a lovely floral pattern. When I inquired about colors, she responded, "pinks and reds." She was becoming more sensitive to everything, including color, so of course the color was stimulating her physically. If her room had been shades of blue, it would have increased her mental level. Or if it had been a yellow and green room, the stimuli would have been emotional. (Chapters Five and Six give more extensive detail on colors.)

A situation like this exemplifies why the Eastern philosophers cautioned people never to increase this awareness without fully understanding it first. It would be like giving someone an airplane to fly before he or she took flying lessons or read the instruction manual.

FIVE

What Color Are You?

*T*his chapter is devoted to the role color plays in our lives and
‑v it affects us. At no time in our lives are we not exposed to color.
‑t look around you and count how many colors are present. If
y're colors you've chosen, have you ever wondered why you
‑cted them? Or if they were selected by someone else, what does
‑ll you about that person?

Before going on any further in this chapter, I'm going to list the
‑en basic colors, with their proven psychological effect.

Red excites the mind and appetite. It represents vitality and
‑creation.

Orange is a combination of red and yellow. It is psychologically
‑rm and cheering, but can also induce overindulgence.

Yellow increases sensitivity by stimulating the central nervous
‑tem. It psychologically inspires and asserts cheerfulness.

Green is the color of healing. Eastern philosophy associates green
‑h the waters of the Earth, which increases harmony of our thoughts
‑d senses.

Blue, considered conservative, encourages restfulness. If you put
‑yperactive child to bed in a room with a blue light bulb burning,
‑vill calm the child and help him or her to sleep.

Indigo (dark blue) produces creativity in people.

Purple is a balance of blue and red. It arouses the inspiration levels from within.

Through the years I've worked with large corporations and schools, recommending colors that would be most suitable for certain areas. This is what I've found. If you want someone to do creative work for you, the best place for him or her to be is in a dark blue or purple room. A yellow and green environment is a good place for people to be cheerful and in harmony with each other. Fast-food restaurants use red, orange, and yellow as their colors, because they evoke a physical response in people. The owners want you to come in, eat, and get out. Their purpose is to fill the place and keep people moving; that's why they're called fast-food restaurants. You react to these colors even if you don't want to.

The color chart is the most important tool I use in my counseling, because it provides me limitless information about a person's energy. I mentioned earlier that everything in our world has an energy field, this field being the program you broadcast. Well, the program must be acted out, and it will affect the relationships and professions you select. According to the energy area you react to the strongest, I'm able to know whether your profession is suitable for you, if you've chosen the right mate, whether you've picked a compatible business partner, if you've selected the right employee. The chart gives me information about your emotional and physical stresses, or things that you're not working on that may cause stress. Are you forcing yourself into being something you're not? Are you overly stressed in some areas? Do your friends or spouse misunderstand you? Do you mis-understand them?

The human body has seven response centers, or chakras, as they are known in Eastern philosophy. When I began investigating the role of intuition, I heard about these things called chakras, and I couldn't fully comprehend them. After a period of study and working with doctors, I realized these seven chakras are our seven endocrine glands. Suddenly, the Eastern philosophy made sense to me. Each response center, or gland, is stimulated by a specific color and musical note. A certain musical tone gives off the same vibration as a specific color. For example, science has proven that a person exposed to the color blue will experience a slowed heartbeat and pulse. It calms the person down just as the musical note G does.

People react to these programs on one of three levels: physical, emotional, or mental. (See the color chart for details.) If a child is a physical reactor and feels his or her mother is yelling about something he or she didn't do, that child will kick the table, pull a sister's hair, or hit the cat in physical frustration. The emotional child will mirror the mother's program. He or she will be snappish with everyone, even a friend, until that program has subsided. The mental child will say, "Hey, I didn't do anything wrong, so what's Mother's problem?" Each child's potential is directed by his or her inborn response to the world. Unfortunately, our school systems haven't found a way of recognizing and dealing with children who react differently to the same situation.

Let's look at the corporate world. The president of a large corporation is distraught because a department of the business has failed to complete a project by its due date. The president reprimands the department head. After leaving the president's office, the department head feels it wasn't his or her fault and passes that same program on to the other people in the department. Like dropping a pebble in a lake—the circles increase and spread. By the end of the day, most of the employees leave work in an angry, discontented mood.

The physical reactor as a child probably would have kicked the manager in the shins, but as an adult he or she knows that that is not acceptable. So he or she slams the telephone down, breaks a pencil in two, and perhaps pounds on the desk. Until the physical reactor gets over it, he or she will want to hit someone but will repress it, slamming doors and desk drawers. He or she will express the anger in physical gestures.

The emotional person will mirror the program he or she just received. If that person was happy earlier, his or her mood will change toward everything. He or she may snap at the nearest person, mirroring the program that was just broadcast to him or her. That person will broadcast those same feelings to people during lunch and perhaps even later at home, until that person can resume his or her program once more.

The mental person is the lucky one. He or she will make a checklist for the situation: **1.** Was it something I did or didn't do? **2.** I wasn't the cause of it. **3.** It was nothing I've done, so I won't worry about it. **4.** I'm just going to stay out of the manager's way until he or she calms down.

That person will go along with his or her day unperturbed. The mental person knows this problem doesn't really involve him or her and realizes there's nothing he or she can do to change it.

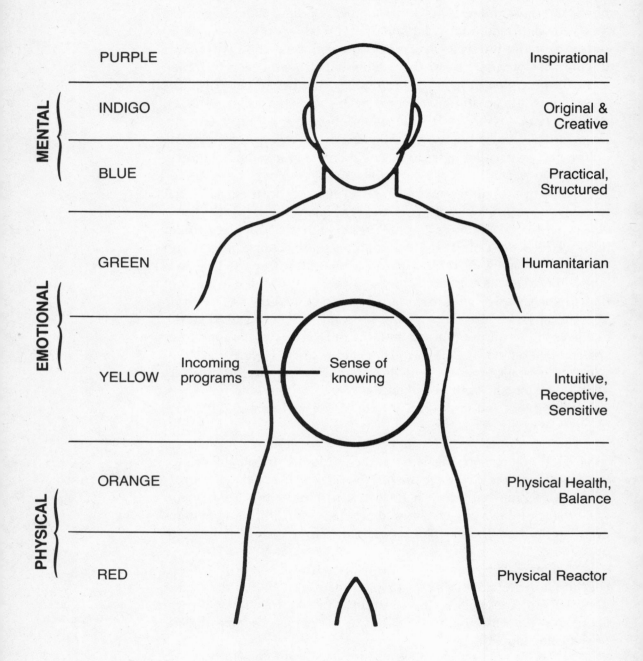

PURPLE — Inspirational

MENTAL
INDIGO — Original & Creative
BLUE — Practical, Structured

GREEN — Humanitarian

EMOTIONAL
YELLOW — Intuitive, Receptive, Sensitive

Incoming programs — Sense of knowing

PHYSICAL
ORANGE — Physical Health, Balance
RED — Physical Reactor

REACTIONS

Do you know what color or colors you are? Do you know why you have a particular reaction to colors? Study the color chart and then read the descriptions. In this chapter you will begin to recognize yourself and understand why you react in certain ways. By the end of the book you will be able to chart yourself and the people around you.

RED

The vibrant color red, in its purest form, rules a physical response center; a red person is a physical reactor. The woman in red is someone men are always attracted to, because it evokes a sexual response. As a homicide detective said in one of my courses, "That's right! You never hear of a blue light district. It's always red."

This color is related to survival and reproduction. The musical note that complements it is C. If our sex glands or physical responses are unhealthy, their energy will be muddied and weak. Nutritionally, vitamin E has been found to be good for the glands connected with red, especially for athletes and others whose work requires great physical stamina. This is why certain people are attracted to red. They find it stimulating and sometimes appropriate for a situation.

During a law enforcment seminar I was teaching, a detective in the back of the room called out, "My wife's been in Europe a couple of months. Do you think that's why I'm painting our bedroom red?"

In the description of orange, you will find a list of some of the professions that are suited for the person who is a physical reactor.

Have you ever heard someone say, "I was so angry, I saw red." Well, uncontrolled rage is red too. It rules everything that is exclusively physical. Some states have found that changing the flashing lights on police cars from red to blue has decreased the arguments between police officers and motorists. The red stimulated both the officers and the drivers, but the blue calmed them down. It has also been proven that a red car exceeding the speed limit will be noticed faster than a car of a different color. Does the police officer seeing your red car physically want to chase you, or does your having a red car cause you to drive faster?

Let's look at another example. You have ten guests over for a sumptuous dinner. After several courses your guests are satisfied, but you want to finish off the meal with a dessert. You serve each guest a dish of vanilla ice cream. A few people might pick at it, but most would leave it untouched. If you placed a red maraschino cherry on top, however, the physical impulse to pick up a spoon and eat a bit would be much greater.

A case that I worked on in San Francisco involved a woman who had been murdered and left in the trunk of her car. She had then been driven over to another part of the neighborhood. To her neighbors, she was outwardly quiet. "A reserved woman," they told the detectives. "No, no, no," I said. "She had some kinky sex partners." I described a local bar she used to frequent, and the puzzled detectives began reinvestigating. They talked with the bartender, who gave them the names of her friends. They visited one of them and got out of his house as soon as they could. The guy had cemented the ceilings and walls of various rooms to make them look like caves and then lit them with different colored lights.

When they called me up to take a look at the house she had lived in, I found her bedroom had a red carpet, red bedspread, red drapes, and red pillowcases. That was where she had been killed. The murderer was reacting to physical urges.

Red will create a physical response in you, even if you're not a physical reactor. And if you are physical reactor, you will react much quicker.

ORANGE

In many ways orange is like red (being a combination of red and yellow), but it represents the physical and sexual, with emotion added. It rules the hormones in both sexes. This response center perceives other people's emotions and gives and receives physical feelings. Its corresponding musical note is D. What is nourishing for red and yellow will also nourish orange.

A young man who had been taking one of my courses for a month came into class one night and shared with me an incident he'd just experienced. While standing in a long line at the IRS, he had looked across the room and noticed a woman surrounded by orange energy. With his newfound interest in people's colors, he walked over, tapped her on the shoulder, and said, "Excuse me, ma'am, but are you experiencing hormonal problems?" Her first reaction was one of great indignation, after which she replied, "As a matter of fact, I am. But I don't know what business it is of yours."

As a counselor, when I see orange instead of red, I look for a health problem or an imbalance in the person's glandular system. Red is a purely physical reaction, whereas orange is more of a physical imbalance in the body's health. Anyone with hormonal imbalances or fluctuations in any of the seven endocrine glands will show an off-color orange in this center. I can always pick out women who are taking birth control pills, menstruating, or pregnant, or have had a hysterectomy. Also, anything that causes a man to worry about his manhood or a woman to question her femininity will throw orange out of balance.

Physical reactors are often athletes, writers, sculptors, chefs, painters, designers, surgeons, gardeners, builders, actors, engineers, or architects. People who work with their hands and want to express themselves physically are part of this group.

If you are a physical reactor and work in a profession that doesn't allow you to express yourself physically, you should take up a sport or hobby such as jogging, painting, woodworking, weightlifting, or dancing—something that allows you to use that energy. If you cut it off, you will hold all your emotional responses to the world within yourself, and that will create problems.

YELLOW

Yellow is the on switch for your intuitive television. It is how you receive and respond to other people and their programs. A "gut feeling" is yellow. Whether good or bad news, fear, love, hate, jealousy, greed, nervousness, or anger, a yellow person feels strong emotions first in the stomach. A key to handling this response center is to be able to filter out what you don't want to receive and to absorb what you do want.

Physically, yellow controls the digestive and assimilative systems, the pancreas, and the adrenals. The related musical note is E. Nutrients that have been found to assist in this area are vitamins A and C, potassium, some enzymes, amino acids, and hydrochloric acid. Highly sensitive people who don't know how to handle their sensitivity have often depleted some or all of these. Prolonged stress or extensive use of the adrenals may cause an inability to assimilate protein, calcium, iron, or the B vitamins.

Yellow is the favorite color for kitchens. I can understand why. A woman (or perhaps a man in today's world) awakening from a night's sleep, having to suddenly face the day's demands, will find he or she is much more sensitive to his or her family, much more attuned than if he or she started the day in a blue kitchen. Being surrounded by the yellow kitchen will cause a person to be a high receiver, even if he or she usually is not. Yellow stimulates reception, enabling a person to anticipate the demands of the day and the family.

Those who work with this response center will find they react strongly when overexposed to yellow. Although it is statistically true that many people prefer a yellow kitchen, I know it is the least desirable color for me. As a Navy wife who moved into many homes with yellow kitchens, I found I always needed to grab a can of green paint and calm the room down. I normally like to awaken and get the feeling of my day before opening up to everyone else's programs.

For me, yellow is good only in rooms where I spend a limited amount of time. People who are already highly sensitive should stay away from it, and please don't paint your children's rooms yellow unless you want them to stay up all night. It would be like putting them to sleep in rooms with televisions blaring.

The yellow response combined with any other color enhances a person's ability. The higher your score here, the more successful you can become.

GREEN

The emotions are seated in green, the response center of humanitarians. These people have great empathy with their surroundings, and feel love and compassion for others. They can feel as intensely about someone else's program as they do about their own. This is the person who will listen to a friend who is having marital problems and take on the problems with the same emotional stress as if they were his or her own problems. This person wants to make life more pleasant for everyone.

This area responds to the musical note F. An imbalance in the area can come about from physical problems with the heart or any buildup of emotional stress. I have seen cases where green was out of balance in a person for a long while because of a "broken heart," and the person eventually developed physical problems with the heart as well.

"Nosey" neighbors can have an imbalance in green, also. They're the people who you might think are minding everyone's business. They're not really. They're just very empathetic and want to hear everyone's story and help them out if they can. It makes them feel good to discuss other people's problems with them and give advice, even sometimes when people are not asking for it. They're the ones standing on the corners, insisting on helping others across the street, even when the others aren't going that way. Those who don't have professions that allow them to give vent to this response can become a nuisance when they just mean to help. They are interested in everyone's life. This leads not only to rejections by people who want to express their own autonomy but also to a weakened person who compulsively serves others to the detriment of his or her own life.

Green people will usually choose a field related to living things. It drives them crazy to be seated in an office pushing paper. Inanimate objects hold no interst for them. They want to work with the living: plants, animals, or people. They make excellent teachers, doctors, nurses, salespeople, attorneys, therapists, veterinarians, horticulturists, florists, farmers, tour guides, animal breeders, and animal trainers. Remember, this is only a partial list for you emotional reactors.

BLUE

Basic blue is strongly related to the practical mental functions, such as following instructions and living a structured day. Blue has been medically proven to slow down the heartbeat and other bodily systems that race under stress. It is found in the thyroid area. Perhaps that's why blue people don't tend to be extensive conversationalists. Blue is a natural tranquilizer, and I feel calcium is related to it, because it has similar tranquilizing properties. Magnesium, protein, and B-complex vitamins nourish the blue area. Its musical note is G.

People who are basic blues can seem nitpicky, but they are dependable and will carry out orders without swaying from them. They are the faithful employees who will work for a company until they receive the gold watch. They are good as students, because they will do things just as the teacher wants them to. Following instructions is what they do best, and they take pride in it; every company needs these people. A routine is comfortable, makes them feel secure.

Very seldom in my years of counseling have I found a person who is all basic blue. It seems to be a color that's most often mixed with other colors. Blues make good accountants, secretaries, technicians, students, office managers, domestic help, cashiers, laborers, and sometimes teachers. Anyone exceptional in one of these fields and not happy doing the job the way someone else tells him or her, has blue mixed with indigo.

INDIGO

Creative thinking and original concepts are associated with indigo, which is located at the forehead. It is related to the pineal gland, and its musical note is A. An indigo person is someone who says, "All right. So you built a mousetrap. I can build a better one." They're not competitive; they just feel another one can be created that works better. They like to improve upon the way things work, create different ways of making things more efficient or more interesting.

Indigo people think for themselves. The physician who is not happy treating an illness the same way it was taught in school will find a better way to control or cure the same illness. An engineer who thinks creatively will find a new design or different way of designing equipment. Being an idea person, an indigo person isn't happy working in a situation that is repetitious or restrictive, allowing little leeway for creativity.

Usually indigo is mixed with another color. An artist, writer, or creative engineer will have it mixed with red, physical energy. The research doctor will have it mixed with green, emotional energy. Indigo people take their creative ideas and apply them with physical or emotional energy.

The indigo person can normally be found in advertising, design, invention, scientific research, technology, education, public relations, philosophy, psychiatry, business consulting, music, the creative arts, or most any profession where a person can find ways of doing the same thing differently, more effectively. He or she doesn't want to work a day that has been planned for him or her. Some geniuses are indigo, but the indigo is usually mixed with purple.

PURPLE

The purple person is an inspired individual. He or she may come up with a totally different idea, such as a revolutionary theory or invention. This response area is connected with the pituitary gland. It responds to the musical note B.

Nobel Prize winners, Albert Einstein, and people such as Leonardo da Vinci, who was drawing airplanes hundreds of years before the Wright brothers, worked from this area. Great religious leaders resonate in purple. People who work in purple are usually ahead of their time. They create works of art, devise inventions, and give us philosophies that we may not fully understand for hundreds of years.

Some purple people may live in purple all the time, preferring to be locked in their daydreams and never bringing their ideas into physical existence. They could be perfectionists or idealists who see the world through rose-colored glasses and find it difficult to live in this world because of its defects. They lose touch with reality because they expect too much from their relationships and the imperfect world around them.

Dr. Jonas Salk took his inspiration and brought it into being, just as Christopher Columbus, Frank Lloyd Wright, Alexander Graham Bell, and the many others who rank with them did. An *idea* without a *happening* is useless.

BLENDING

Most everyone's program incorporates more than one color. Usually you will find three or more: one is the strongest and the others are supporting responses. Sometimes a person will work from a supporting response, but the others will also be influential. How the colors blend determines what you are most effective at professionally, and who will complement your life personally.

Take doctors. Green is normally their strongest color, because they have a need to help people. Doctors who are basic blue and green will make good general practitioners, follow their medical training to a T, and be content making their patients comfortable. But I've charted doctors whose main color was indigo or purple. They were interested in what they could do new and different in science and found their background in science allowed them to practice their creativity in the medical field. Doctors who are indigo and green will not be satisfied with following the same routine each day, as their interest is to find new ways of practicing and researching medicine. Doctors who are purple and green can become great leaders, perfecting advanced technologies in medicine. Yellow-and-indigo or yellow-and-purple doctors will be at the top of their profession, because they add intuition to a medical intellect, providing more and quicker answers than others.

Let's take artists, the red reactors. If they have basic blue, they will be happy just splashing paint on a canvas or molding any type of sculpture so they can enjoy the physical release. Artists of green and red will tend to paint familiar images, scenes everyone can relate to; examples of such artists are Norman Rockwell and Andrew Wyeth. Artists with indigo will produce works that are original. Their works will excite us even though they may not relate explicitly to our own lives. Purple artists are da Vinci, Van Gogh, and Dali. Not everyone understands at the time what they are creating, but years later, people consider them to be great.

Let's look at the lawyer working with green and basic blue. That person is going to advise people with legal facts, operate out of an office, and be very happy working that way. Throw a little red in, and he or she will be working in court, using theatrics to explain a case to the jury. That attorney is effective with physical expression. The indigo attorney will write new laws or become known as tops in this profession.

The worst thing you could do to a humanitarian would be to lock him or her in a room with nothing to do but push paper around all day. He or she needs to interact with others. It would be the same as tying the hands of an artist, leaving him or her to think all day. An artist must put it down, work feelings and ideas out so he or she can see them and feel them with the body.

Something to ask yourself about your profession is whether you were pushed into it because that's what your parents wanted you to do, whether finances forced you to undertake it, or whether it's really what you want to do. If you are working at something unfit for you, then you must realize that that adds stress to your life and the lives of people around you.

An accountant came to me for counseling following my appearance on television in Los Angeles. I noticed he emanated a tremendous amount of green energy. I told him I would never put him in an office doing something as repetitious as accounting, because he was a people person, not a paper person. He said, " You know, you're right. I've always wanted to be a psychologist." After discussing this, it became clear to him why he had carried so much stress through his life and how his program of unfulfillment had been picked up by his entire family. After his session with me, he turned his accounting firm over to his partner and returned to college, earning a degree in psychology. The last time I saw him, the stress was gone and he was smiling.

One way to find out what blend of colors you are is to look at the mental, emotional, and physical aspects of yourself. Be very honest and ask yourself, If I had to give up one, working with my head, working with people, or working with my body, which would be the easiest to give up? That is your last, or number 3, area. The one you could give up next is a secondary response. The response you feel would be hardest to give up is the primary one. If you find two would be impossible to give up, they are 1A and 1B, rather than 1 and 2. The other is 2 instead of 3. Don't make the mistake of putting yourself in the mental area first because that makes you feel more intelligent. It has nothing to do with your level of intelligence. It has to do only with the area from which you enjoy working. Your main color could be green and you could be smarter than the blue person.

Let's look at my children's colors.

Charles, my youngest son, is a combination of 1) red, 2) indigo, and 3) green. He is a strong physical reactor with a creative mind, which he wanted to use in helping people. He was captain of a water polo team, and worked with children, teaching them swimming and life saving. He wanted to be a medical doctor, but he crewed at UCLA, which prevented him from earning all As and also prevented his entrance into medical school. He's a terrific humanitarian with a lot of physical energy, both of which are required in a pediatrician. He was always doing something with children, and would have been excellent as a children's doctor, but our school system doesn't look to see if a person has all the ingredients to fulfill its degree; it looks to see if a person has straight As. Now he works as a biochemist and recently received his master's in business. It makes me worry, because he may end up pushing paper and not have the physical release he needs. Fortunately he does scuba dive, swim, and jog.

Christopher is 1) a combination of blue and indigo, 2) green, and 3) red. My middle son is always thinking of ways he can make more money. He tries to make a better mousetrap, design something original. He enjoys cerebral work, and has been an honor student since the fifth grade. He works out at the gym because it's healthy, not because he feels the need to do it. He's physical to an extent, but he's not compulsive about it. He's the indigo person who's always thinking, but he uses the blue to make it practical and work for him.

Then we have Bill, the oldest boy. Though he's an electrical engineer, coming out of the red, he's always designing, using his indigo and purple. I can remember when he was not more than three or four, I woke up in the middle of the night to the sound of the dishwasher running, toaster popping toast, radio and television blaring, and the clothes washer running. Literally everything electrical in the house was operating at the same time. He had to find out how things worked. Even at the age of two, when a new appliance was delivered to the house, he would squat down, watch it being installed, and then try to run it. Once when he was seven, I arrived home to find him standing outside in the winter weather. He had a large dry-cell battery hooked to a wooden box in the front yard. I asked him what he was doing, and he said, "Building a hothouse." Neither his father nor I had ever discussed or taken him to a hothouse, so I said, "That's nice. What are you going to do with it?" "I'm going to grow peas." "Well, where are you going to get the seeds for the peas?" He smiled. "Out of my pea shooter." And, sure enough, he did grow peas. He went from solving technical problems for everyone in the neighborhood to becoming a design engineer for new products. Color him 1) purple/indigo, 2) red, and 3) green. He's happiest exploring the ways of the mind.

Cindy's colors are 1) purple, 2) red, and 3) green. She's creative and far out. As a child she always had to be outdoors. She named every squirrel and bird in the neighborhood, concocting wonderful stories about their lives. This was her purple mixed with red. But her main energy is purple with indigo. She taught herself to play the guitar and the piano, often writing her own music and lyrics. As a child she preferred to lock herself in her room to draw and write than play with others. A couple hours of play, and she was back to her creativity. And when in her creative mode, she was unaware of anyone else. Her mind is always working in a creative way.

Although all of them come from the same family, there are many combinations going on. Each one of them has green, but they respond to it differently. It's the same with you. You have your own program and you need to react to it for self-fulfillment in your work and personal life. After all, we are all individuals.

SIX

How to Exercise Your Intuition

Okay, you've heard the theory; now it's time to get your feet wet. This second half of the book is where you learn how to get in touch with and really become acquainted with your own intuition. If possible, ask a friend or family member to share these experiences with you, as you can provide each other with material to work on as well as an immediate response. The information on your progress allows you to know the accuracy of your feelings and how well you apply them. And after you've practiced the exercises, it's great fun to try them around the dinner table with your family.

Materials needed for the exercises in the second half of this book:

1. One deck of regular playing cards.

2. Poster board, which is a type of thin white cardboard, and can be purchased in packages of 7 by 11 inches or as one large sheet. Pieces of poster board will be glued to the backs of some of your playing cards. Other pieces will be used for the seven colors and the exercise on shapes. See the instructions at the beginning of each section.

3. Seven pieces of colored construction paper, one in each of the seven colors discussed in Chapter Five.

4. One thick black marker pen.

You can purchase poster board and colored construction paper at all art stores. You may even find them at your local drugstore or where school supplies are sold.

TUNING UP

In the beginning, select a room or place that encourages relaxation. The room should be comfortable and used at a time of day when there are the least number of distractions. At first you want to subdue anything that could affect one of your other senses until this state becomes familiar. After a while, you will be able to do this, as I can, in the middle of Times Square. It's like learning to play the piano. At first you are painfully aware of hitting each note. After plenty of practice, you can play a concerto thinking of the notes not as separate but as part of the whole piece.

When I first began to get in touch with my own intuition, I pulled the drapes, unplugged the telephone, and told my children not to make a sound. It took that much effort just to relax. Now I can get in touch with that feeling whenever and wherever, because it is so familiar to me.

As we discussed earlier in the book, color and musical notes have an effect on you, physically, emotionally, and mentally. We are going to use the same colors and notes discussed in Chapter Five in an exercise for relaxation. It is not only for relaxing, but will also enable you to analyze what's happening in your life. Begin with the following steps.

1. Find a quiet room in which you can relax and set your other five senses aside.

2. In the back of the book is an insert with the seven colors on it. Hang this visual aid on the wall in the room you will be using.

3. Be sure to avoid distractions of any sort, such as the continual taste of the onions you had for lunch, the sound of noisy construction going on outside, the smell of dinner cooking in the kitchen, the sight of anything distracting in the room, or the feel of tight clothing.

4. Proceed through the seven colors and notes to reach a state of complete relaxation, using relaxation sequence number one.

The first several times you do this exercise, visualize only a color. After you become familiar with that part of the exercise, you can then add the musical notes to intensify each step. In class I use a specifically designed cassette tape of the associated notes in a sequence that is made just for the exercise and 35mm slides of each color, which can be projected on a wall or screen. I use the tape and slides for class because they project more impact than just the poster.*

Now that you have gotten yourself set up and comfortable, begin by visualizing the color red. Remember, red is a pure physical color and it is at the bottom of the spectrum. As you sit comfortably, look at your chart to see where the red applies to the physical body. You want the color in its pure form, not an orange, pink, or muddy red.

---

*If you would like to use the colored slides and accompanying cassette tape that I use in class you will need the following equipment:

1. A 35mm slide projector.

2. A cassette tape player.

3. A sheet of Mylar (not plastic) stage gels in each of the seven colors (red, orange, yellow, green, blue, indigo and purple.) These gels are used for stage lighting and can be found at any theatrical equipment and supplies company. Be sure you or the salesperson selects pure colors in each gel. If you do not find a theatrical equipment company in your city then perhaps the local stage group can help you. Most large cities have supply companies.

4. A set of 35mm empty slides in which you can mount the gels. These are found in local photo supply stores. Cut each gel so it fits into the slide and secure them according to instructions that come with the box of empty slide frames. You now have a set of seven colored slides to place in order of color in your projector.

5. This may be the most difficult step but don't give up. You want to record a cassette tape with the seven musical notes to be used with your colors and in the same sequence. Begin with middle C, D, E, F, G, A, and B. This can be done by using a piano, organ, or any instrument in the piano family. Perhaps even a child's toy

Then in your mind visualize the color in that area of your body. If you want to close your eyes, visualize the color red coming in and totally filling the room. Feel that you're being wrapped in the color, totally immersed physically and mentally. Let the color engulf your entire body and ask yourself how red makes you feel. How comfortable or uncomfortable are you with the color? Are you tired? If so, have you been physically too busy lately? Or are you suppressing a physical response, such as anger?

Always stay with the color until you feel comfortable being surrounded by it, even if you are not a physical reactor. In the beginning it will take you longer to work through each color. When I use the slides in class, I usually keep the students two minutes with each color. Sometimes we work through the spectrum more than once before everyone is completely comfortable. And I recommend the students wear light cotton clothing so the color can more easily penetrate. It has been proven that the wavelengths given off by any color pass through pure cotton easier than a synthetic material. It's the same as when a mountain blocks a channel's wavelength, causing a television not to receive clearly.

When you've finished with the color red, slowly move up to orange and do the same thing. Again, really concentrate on filling

---

piano. A flute or harmonica could also be used for the seven simple notes needed. You want to start and tape the notes in sequence, beginning with the middle C for red and continuing up the scale one note for each color. I used an oscillator so I am able to hold the note for the two minutes I remain with each color. But if you are using a musical instrument, then you may just hit each note and hold it until it fades away, leaving the remainder of the two minutes blank on the tape so you do not hear the next note until you have spent two munites with the last color—or you might continue hitting the note for the duration of the two minutes. I leave this up to your creativity.

6. Set up your projector and cassette player so that while you relax with each color, you have to exert minimum effort in changing the color as you go from one to another. If you don't happen to have a screen, then use a white wall to display the colors. The larger the surface, the more you feel enveloped in that particular color.

This may sound like an enormous amount of work, but it only takes a little ingenuity. If a projector is not available, you may make your cassette tape and use with the color inserts that you find in this book. The slides and tape can be used as a relaxing exercise for the children before bed or the adults after a long hard day. Just use Relaxation Sequence Number One for this purpose.

*How to Exercise
Your Intuition*

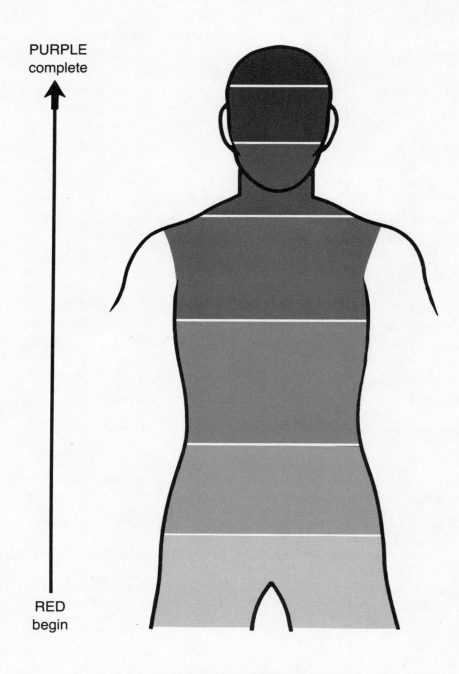

PURPLE
complete

RED
begin

COLOR & TONE TECHNIQUES

RELAXATION SEQUENCE Number One

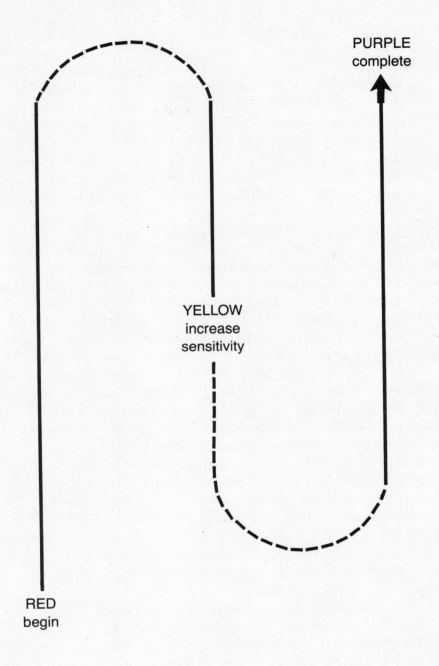

PURPLE
complete

YELLOW
increase
sensitivity

RED
begin

RELAXATION SEQUENCE Number Two

your mind and body with the color. If you get a mixture or muddy orange, stay with the exercise until you bring in and visually hold the pure color. If you're uncomfortable with orange, it means something is wrong or in a state of fluctuation with the physical body. Do you still have a touch of the flu? Are you menstruating, or pregnant?

Work through the remaining five colors in the same way, noting if anything feels uncomfortable. If yellow is difficult, perhaps you've been too sensitive to people. Are you tired of feeling other people's problems? Have you eaten too much sugar and overstressed your adrenals? The green is your empathetic color. It could be disturbed if you feel people are not caring about you. Is your spouse being insensitive? If either of the blues seem impure or difficult to visualize, then maybe you have been doing too much mental work. Are you attempting to avoid or block out your own knowledge of any facts?

The color and tone exercise is something you do whenever you want to relax yourself and sit down to chat with your intuition. It's the exercise that washes away all other programs and carries them downstream, so you can get back in touch with your own program. It can be used to help you unwind just before going to sleep or to help you clear your thoughts in the morning. One group of medical professionals with whom I worked listened to the tape and visualized the colors while driving to their jobs. So if you don't have time for the color exercise before leaving for work, you can do it on the way to work. Just don't run through red stop signs!

Anytime a color gives you difficulty during the exercise, make a checklist to find out why it bothers you. After you've done the exercise many times, you can begin to analyze and diagnose yourself daily, becoming your own psychologist. Imagine, for example, that on a given day you find it difficult to bring red into focus or it makes you agitated. Then you want to analyze your day. Have you had too much physical activity? Have you been suppressing physical responses to things, such as wanting to punch your boss in the nose? Are you a physical reactor who hasn't gotten out and exercised lately? If the physical colors are okay, but green or yellow gives you trouble, look at the emotional aspects of your life. Do you have some emotional issues you haven't solved? Is there a problem in a relationship that you haven't really faced? What's really going on in your life emotionally? If you have problems with the mental colors, have you been doing too much paperwork or too much cerebral work this week?

I was once asked by a psychiatrist if I would present my color and tone exercise at one of his workshops for his patients. Before then I hadn't used it specifically for this type of group. After everyone was seated, we began with the color red. There was much unease and discomfort among the people. The feelings were so strong in the area of the room to my left that I stopped projecting the color. I turned to the woman sitting there and gently asked her if there was any reason I would feel a strong aversion from her to the color red. She replied in a very controlled and tightlipped way, "No." So that she wouldn't feel like she was being singled out, I then turned to the group on my right and selected one young man. Asking him, "Are you aware that you are a physical reactor? Even if you have to sit at a desk all day, I highly recommend that you go out after work and find a sport or hobby that allows you to give vent to your physical reactions to the world."

The young man smiled. "You're really right. I'm a law student and at the end of the day I'm fidgeting. Can't wait to exercise my body."

Just as I was changing the slide to the color orange, a little voice piped up in the darkened room from where the woman on my left was sitting. "Well, I do have epilepsy." To me, epilepsy manifests itself in the physical reaction of not being able to handle things. Very often an epileptic seizure transpires when a person is overly distraught. Her feeling of aversion had been so strong that I had had to stop and discuss the situation with the woman.

The group moved through the physical colors also with a great deal of tension in the room. When we moved up into yellow and green, the emotions in the room were so thick that it made for an extremely uncomfortable feeling for everyone. The emotions were circling and crashing into one another like bumper cars at a carnival. I leaned over to the doctor and asked if he could feel it. There was no way you could ignore it.

We switched to the blues and the feeling shifted so drastically that it was like everyone was breathing a sigh of relief after having over-come dangerous waters. Now they were in their heads and only had to think. Everything was peaceful. But afterward I realized that the doctor had busied himself with teaching people to rationalize and think out their problems, but that they had still not mastered their physical and emotional responses. As long as these people operated on a mental level, they were fine. But how does a person stay in balance if he or she deals with a problem on only one of three levels?

I say, "That person can't."

One evening a student came into the classroom. He had always come straight from his graphic design company, where he did creative things, and walked into the room with a beautiful indigo floating in behind him. But this night he came roaring into class, barely making it on time, and carrying nothing but red energy. I had to ask, "What happened? Why the sudden change?"

He explained that while driving to class, he had had his foot heavy on the gas pedal, and the man in blue with the flashing red lights had stopped him. That particular officer had not been willing to listen to reason, the end result was one big fat ticket. The guy came into the room still wishing he had given the cop one big fat lip. It took him two times through the color exercise before he could get rid of all his anger.

A class of twenty people who come together after having worked through programs on different levels all day—green, blue, red, purple, all kinds—takes a while to get in unison. And if there is one person broadcasting a strong physical program, students may not make it up to the purple. Or if one person is broadcasting a strong green program, the class may get hung up on that color. Sometimes a class will go smoothly through the exercise, and other times a person will play his or her broadcast of a bad day again and again, until everyone has heard it. That person is just not willing to let it go and change the group dynamics. This is something to think about if you plan to work with a friend. Your program can affect your friend and vice versa.

Remember, it's advantageous to work with someone if possible. If you have a partner, it would be very good for him or her also to sit down and go through the colors, so you'll both be more relaxed prior to the exercises. Also remember not to let your wishful thinking or thoughts about the other person interfere with your receiving information.

Once you're relaxed and you want to turn your television on for receiving other programs, work back down through the colors. Start with purple and hold it for one minute, than move into indigo and hold it. Normally once you've gone up the color chart, it's easy to go back down. Continue down through blue, through green, and then into yellow. Hold yellow for a minute and stop there with the colors.

Okay, now we've discussed that relaxation is important for the exercises. It's necessary to subdue everything that could intrude on the other senses. Once you've reached that point and have worked through the colors and notes, you're ready to exercise your intuition, flex your intuitive muscles. Always remember that there are no As or Fs for doing the exercises. This is an experience of describing and interpreting your own feelings. It's like creating a new recipe. You must add ingredients until it tastes right to you. Don't forget to describe your feelings aloud so you can understand them better.

CARDS

Most of you probably already have playing cards around the house. You can get a great deal of mileage from them. Try to select a deck that doesn't have a distracting color or pattern on the back. If it does, paste a piece of white poster board over that side, so the color and pattern will not visually interfere during this exercise. You will find a personal progress chart following this exercise that you can fill in to monitor your progress.

The first thing you are going to do is discover what the color red feels like. You've *seen* it many times but you've probably never stopped to realize what it *felt* like. Take your deck and pull out some of the red cards. Don't use the face cards at this time; you will use them later. Lay the cards face up on the table so that all you see is red. Now get in touch with what red feels like to you. Try different words and say them out loud to see what fits. Is it energetic, vibrant, powerful, irritating, or hot? Or is it some entirely unrelated word?

As I mention in *The Psychic Is You,* don't assume everyone reacts in the same way to a color, so get yourself to really describe the feeling. Spend the time you need to realize red actually creates a certain feeling in you. Once you've reached the point of believing you know what the color red feels like, then move on to the black. Repeat the same procedure with black. Is it heavy, light, empty, cold, a void, depressing, sophisticated? Each person must build his or her own vocabulary of responses, and the more accurately you describe each feeling for yourself, the more accurate your results will be. Take your time and search out the description. This is an exercise of feeling, and feelings are not something to rush.

Once you have described and differentiated the feelings of red and black, have your partner remove one of each from the deck and hold them so you can't see their colors. When you feel the colors, select which is red and which is black. When working by yourself, select several cards of each color. Put them face down on the table in front of you and move them around, with your eyes closed, to ensure that you no longer know the identity of each card.

You may have immediately felt which card was red and which was black. If so, you're the kind of person who probably has used your intuition so often that it immediately sends a signal to your intellect and you just know which color it is. If, however, you are uncomfortable with your first feeling, here are other ways you can reach a conclusion:

1. Picture the card in your mind. Then see yourself turn the card over and see which color fills your eyes.

2. Mentally project the color red on the card and feel whether it fits. Before you decide, project the color black on the same card, and then feel whether it fits better. Try this several times until you are sure which feels right.

3. Use your sense of touch. Remember, any of the five senses can be used in conjunction with your intuition. So place a black card and a red card on the table face down. Put your hand on one, and then on the other. Feel the differences and identify them. Does the red one feel warmer or lighter? Does the black one feel colder or heavier?

You can also do the same thing with the shape of the suit. What you want to do is define and identify the shape. Begin with one card of each suit lying face up on the table. Get in touch with how they feel to you. In this exercise you can combine your sense of touch and intuition to help you define the feelings transmitted by each shape. Draw the shape with your hands out in front of you while describing the feelings aloud. Your intuition will tell you when your hands outline the shape.

1. What does a heart feel like to you? Is it smooth, pointed, rounded?

2. What does a diamond feel like to you? Is it straight lines instead of rounded? Is it sharp?

3. Go on to the black suits. Notice the differences between a club and a spade. Draw a spade with your hands. Draw a club with your

hands. How would they feel if you were to reach out and intuitively touch them? Would the club be more lumpy and the spade flow more smoothly?

I will always remember the expression on a particular police captain's face during a weekend law enforcement seminar I gave in Santa Barbara. The seminar included representatives from the FBI, the Secret Service, arson squads, sheriff's offices, and police departments from all over California. On the second day, after we had discussed theory, I gave them several different cases to solve. First they were shown a photograph of the criminal. From the picture they were to intuitively tell the type of crime the person had committed, the number of people involved, the type of weapon used, and the type of vehicle driven.

I had told them they could reach out and touch the shape of the vehicle. After three or four cases in which cars were used, I threw them a curve by giving them a case in which a pickup truck was used. This captain, who was sitting in the second row, drew the outline of a car in the air in front of him. I watched as he drew another shape of a car. Then he started drawing a flat outline, taking his hands and making a flat motion in the air several times. He went back and tried the shape of a car again. Then he drew the flat line again, looked at me, and asked, "It's not a pickup truck, is it?" And I said, "Yes." Excitement animated his face. "I could feel it! I could feel the difference between the outline of a car and the outline of the truck."

This is what I want you to understand. You could intuitively feel the card lying in front of you if I asked you to draw it. What kind of shape does it take? What does it feel like to your hands? This shape will always be the shape it feels most natural to draw.

The next thing you're going to do is work with the number on each card. Take a look at a card, let's say the four of hearts: there are four hearts on the center of that card. The six of hearts, of course, has six hearts on it. Work through the process like this:

1. In order to decide the number of the card, you need to decide whether the card has lots of spots of color on it. If so, that's a higher number card. The more color there is, the higher the number of the card.

2. If it feels like a high number, try the number ten. If that doesn't feel

right, intuitively place nine on the card. If that feels better but you're still uncertain, try an eight. If that feels much better, it's probably an eight. You can place and remove the numbers until you feel satisfied. Remember, in the beginning, if you're anywhere within three or four numbers, you should be very happy.

If you work a lot with numbers, you've already formed an intellectual foundation with numbers. You will probably give quicker and more accurate answers than someone who seldom works with them.

The last thing to do with the cards is add the face cards. They usually have more than one color on them and feel more mixed, more congested, than the red or black cards. Define how the face card feels to you, then put one or two of them in with the other cards lying on the table. See if you can pick them out of the red and black cards. Also, if you have a partner, have him or her select eight or ten cards and set the rest of the deck aside. Get your partner to hold one card at a time in front of you, and you tell him or her what it is.

Don't ever let your conscious mind work with odds. I have found in class that when the cards get shuffled, several of the same color may appear together. A person will be very accurate intuitively until the conscious mind comes in and says, "Ah ha! This can't be another black card." These cards are in no particular order, so you might have, for example, seven black ones in a row.

Here are the card exercises I've described, in order:

1. Define the feeling of black and red. Practice identifying these colors while the cards are face down or turned away from you.

2. Take one card from the four suits (no face cards), get a feeling for each shape, and then identify them while they lie face down or in your partner's hand.

3. Practice deciding what number is on the face of the card.

4. Add face cards to the group and pick them out from among the others.

These are basic exercises that will teach you to build and flex your intuitive muscles. Starting with the basics and getting immediate results encourages you to trust your intuition before you begin applying it on more advanced levels. I had one student, an attorney, who found the card exercises helpful with his poker game. After four or five weeks, he came into class beaming because he had won more money than usual. I say, if it helps, use it.

Card Chart

	1	2	3	4	5	6	7	8	9	10	11	12	13	14	15
RED															
BLACK															
HEART															
DIAMOND															
SPADE															
CLUB															
FACE CARD															
LOW NUMBER															
HIGH NUMBER															

Fill in this chart by placing a check by the answer you feel, beginning with card number one, number two, etc. It will help if you make several copies of the charts contained in this book, so that you can continue these exercises and note your progress.

As for me, I always found math my least interesting class, so numbers are not my best intuitive subject because of lack of practice. Oh, I can get a number every so often, but not an entire sequence of numbers. The detectives I work cases with always tease me and say, "Just give us the suspect's social security number, address, or license plate number and we'll be happy." Someday I'm going to surprise them more than I already have.

Here are some daily exercises for sharpening your intuitive sense.

TELEPHONE CALLS

When the telephone rings, ask yourself some of the following questions as you walk to answer it:

1. In your mind's eye do you see yourself talking on the phone? Or do you see yourself handing the phone to another because the call is for someone else?

2. Sense whether it is a man or a woman on the line. You might be surprised at how difficult it is to intuitively decide whether it is a man or a woman. You might think that we would be able to differentiate more easily.

   Find something you can intuitively associate with each sex. What stands out the most in your mind when you think of each sex? Is it the shape of the hands, the head, the hairstyle, the walk, the clothing, or the size of the foot? Whatever you come up with to identify each sex, you should continually use it as a symbol of recognition.

3. Is it an everyday type of call? Or is it from someone you hadn't expected to hear from?

4. Is it long distance or is it a local call?

If you feel like you don't have enough time to answer these questions while walking to the phone, intuit the answers before the telephone rings again. You can answer the questions, determine who the next caller will be, and jot down your answers so you will remember them.

SHORTCUTS FOR SHOPPING

If there is a particular object you're shopping for, select three or four stores where it could be, and intuit at which store you will find it. Intuit the price as well. Then call all the stores for confirmation.

1. Decide which store will have the product.

2. Telephone all of the stores to see which one actually does have the product.

3. Is it the price you had intuited? Higher or lower?

4. Sports—who wins? By how much?

NEWS

While listening to the news, try to intuit outcomes. Following are some suggestions.

1. If several candidates are running for office, intuit who will win.

2. If a trial is in progress, what is the verdict going to be?

3. If a corporation is having financial difficulty, is it going to declare bankruptcy or merge with another?

MAIL

Before your mail carrier arrives, decide what will show up in your mailbox.

1. Are there bills?

2. Is there junk mail?

3. Are there personal letters? If so, do they contain happy news or sad?

4. How many pieces of mail are you going to receive, few or many?

5. Is there anything out of the ordinary such as a notification that you are the winner of a million dollar sweepstakes?

WORK

While driving to work you might pose the following questions:

1. If you don't have an assigned parking space, decide where you'll find one. What street is it on, how far is it from the office, what is its geographical location in relation to the office?

2. Select one person in the office and decide what color he or she is going to wear. Is it a solid color or part of a print? Is it dark or a bright color? As you become familiar with the feelings of different colors, you will be able to be more specific. Choose a different person periodically.

3. Feel the mood a particular person is in before you meet with him or her. Is the person happy or depressed? Is he or she pleased with work or looking for a change?

This exercise can be used daily. It can also be applied to other situations such as social engagements and business appointments. If you take the time, you will find that your daily schedule presents many opportunities for practice. Experiment with using your intuition in ways that are relevant to you.

Doctors, for example, can make a notation about a patient's problem before seeing the patient. Get the feeling of the patient before walking into the examining room. Is the problem physical, mental, or emotional? If physical, in what part of the body will you find the problem?

Attorneys can get a sense about their potential clients. Before a client sees you, intuit answers to the following questions. Do you feel you will accept the case? If so, does the client have all the necessary information, or will you have to spend many hours gathering information? Will the case have to be settled in court? Is it going to be heard by a jury or a judge? Can you win this one easily, with difficulty, or not at all? Be sure to use a combination of intuition and intellect so that you don't give up before you start.

If you are a sales representative, ask yourself some of the following questions before your day begins. How many sales will I complete today? This week? This month? Of the people I contact today, which will buy now, which will buy later, which won't ever buy? Until you feel confident about your intuition, don't ignore those people you feel may not purchase, because you might miss a sale.

In sports, whether you're a team member or a spectator, decide who will be the winner and by how many points. If you go to the races, which horse or dog will place first? Second?

Teachers, make notations at the beginning of each year about your students. Which ones will excel? Which ones will receive average grades? Which ones will need the most help? Before you give a test, intuit the percentage of students that will pass. This may assist you in helping the right students before their problems cause them to lose interest and fail.

You can get a sense of a situation, translate that feeling with your intellect, and check the results against the notes you previously made. Your intellect will automatically merge with the feeling as you translate it. The words my students hate to hear are, Your intuition is the result of practice, not magic. So plug yourself in and practice, practice, practice!

SEVEN

Color Identification

*T*his is a most important exercise, because you will use the information you gain from it over and over when you outline charts on other people regarding how they react to incoming programs, their suitable professions, and their best relationships. The more you can recognize the traits that accompany the seven colors, the more accurate you will be. You will find, when using your intuition about a person, that one of these colors will become apparent to you. Color is a subtle enhancement of a total picture, a tool to help you receive a fuller perception.

Take the colored sheets of construction paper and mount each of them on separate squares of white poster board which has been cut into playing-card size (2½ by 3½ or larger). Later you will be using these as a diagnostic tool to provide information concerning another person. (You've already become your own therapist by using these same colors during the relaxation exercise. Now you're going to learn to apply them in the same manner when you do psychological profiles on other people.)

What you want to do is get in touch with each of the seven colors, red through purple. Is the color physical, emotional, or mental? What reaction does each evoke in you? Discover how each color feels for you and where in your body you feel the reaction. Refer to the color chart in Chapter Five to see whether colors are physical, emotional, or mental, and the part of the body to which each color corresponds.

Now have your partner hold up one of the cards. Or if you're working by yourself, turn several cards face down, mix them up, and then choose one. Following are the different ways you can conclude what color the card is:

1. Ask yourself if the card feels physical, emotional, or mental. Where on your body do you feel it the strongest?

2. Now you've narrowed down the choice of colors. Which do you feel it is?

3. Project the color in your mind and feel if it matches the color of the selected card.

4. If that doesn't work, go through and apply the other colors to find the one it is most likely to be.

After you have practiced this for some time, you will no longer see people as black, yellow, red, or white. Instead they will appear as vibrant shades ranging from red to purple. This will make your world more colorful. Someday you might even hear a friend say, "I'm going to marry the most darling purple person!" Or your employer might exclaim at a departmental meeting, "I just hired a great green person!" In your favorite cocktail lounge, you might overhear a tired voice explaining to a friend, "Yes, I really did like her. But I never could keep up with red people."

Color Chart

	1	2	3	4	5	6	7	8	9	10	11	12	13	14	15
RED															
ORANGE															
YELLOW															
GREEN															
BLUE															
INDIGO															
PURPLE															

Fill in this chart by placing a check by the answer you feel, beginning with color number one, number two, etc. It will help if you make several copies of the charts contained in this book, so that you can continue these exercises and note your progress.

EIGHT

Sensing Shapes

Before you begin this exercise, take six pieces of poster board and cut them to any size you desire, 2½ inches by 3½ inches or larger. Use your black marker pen to outline one of these shapes on each card: circle, square, diamond, triangle, five-pointed star, straight line. These cards are similar to those designed and used by Dr. Rhine in his research on parapsychology at Duke University.

Once more you will combine intuition with the sense of touch.

1. Repeat the procedure of shuffling and mixing the cards, so you don't know which shape is where.

2. Either you or your partner should select a card with which to work.

3. Now use your hands to sense the feeling of the shape. Again, draw the shape in the air. Try each one until you find the shape that feels correct.

4. It might help you to use a pencil and paper to draw the shape you sense is on the card.

At times shapes can play an important role in translating your flashes of intuition. They have given me help in solving some of the law enforcement cases on which I've worked. This exercise can also prove most enjoyable as a family game. And don't be surprised if the younger members of the family, whose intuition has not been buried so deeply, score higher than the adults.

Shape Chart

	1	2	3	4	5	6	7	8	9	10	11	12	13	14	15
CIRCLE															
SQUARE															
DIAMOND															
TRIANGLE															
STAR															
STRAIGHT LINE															

Fill in this chart by placing a check by the answer you feel, beginning with shape number one, number two, etc. It will help if you make several copies of the charts contained in this book, so that you can continue these exercises and note your progress.

NINE

Personal Profile With Pictures

*I*n this chapter you will learn to interpret the programs other people broadcast. Those of you who did not enjoy or feel successful working with inanimate objects may find you excel in this chapter.

In this chapter you will work from pictures selected for this book. The people in the pictures come from different walks of life, and no two personal profiles are the same. You will first decide which of the three areas—mental, emotional, or physical—appears to be each person's primary reaction to life. Beginning with the mental level, make notations on your personal profile chart concerning what you find with each person regarding colors, from purple down through red.

Some questions you might ask yourself are:

Purple—Is the person expressing inspiration periodically, constantly, or not at all?

Indigo—Does the person employ creative thinking in his or her profession or hobbies? (Note that it is possible to find an indigo person who is afraid to trust his or her own creativity.)

Blue—Is blue used by this person to complete ideas from indigo or as a way of structuring life?

Green—Does this person enjoy sharing with people socially or professionally? Or is the person happiest when working with inanimate objects?

Yellow—Do you find the person sensitive and intuitive?

Orange—Does the person have any health problems, whether caused by mental, emotional, or physical factors?

Red—Is the person vital and aggressive?

Other information can be elicited by using this chart. I've found it a valuable tool in counseling regarding career, business partnerships, and personal relationships, as well as in analyzing the motivations of criminals. The more you use this chart the more extensive the information you will receive on the subject. So don't rush. Take your time on each level until you feel you've gathered all pertinent data.

Before this exercise you may find it helpful to reacquaint yourself with the seven colors, appropriate professions for those of different colors, and the color chart in Chapter Five. You may want to make several copies of the chart so you can use one as a personal profile for each person with whom you work. The more you make, the more fun you'll have!

Now relax and don't try too hard. Be satisfied if your intellect translates a few distinct feelings in the beginning. You're on the path of success, because with practice the amount of information you receive will increase.

1. First, work through the colors and decide which is the person's number 1 color. Is the person a physical, emotional, or mental reactor? Does the person work with the hands, the mind, or other people? Remember, the person may be a combination of two or three colors, as described in Blending in Chapter Five.

2. Next, describe what the person looks like.

3. Then, ask yourself questions about the person's marital status. Is the individual single, married, separated, divorced, or widowed? One way I've found that works well in determining this is to put a spouse next to the person in the picture. Does that feel right? Does the spouse remain or disappear from the picture? Another method is to put a wedding band on the finger of the person. Does it stay or does the person remove the ring? If the ring is taken off, look to see if a legal paper has been drawn up. Then

give a physical description of the spouse. What is the hair color? Eye color? Height? Weight?

4. Next, look for any children. How many children does the person have? Use the same method as you did to find the number on the playing cards, adding or subtracting one child at a time until you feel the number is right. What are the sexes of the children? Put dresses on the girls and pants on the boys, or use whatever symbol you like to distinguish between boys and girls.

5. What animals does the person have: cats, dogs, birds, reptiles, or livestock? Try different sizes, colors, and fur textures. How many animals are there?

6. Now list the personality traits of the subject. Is the person friendly, gregarious, reserved, or aggressive? Does he or she have a sense of humor or a stern personality? Try different expressions on the person's face. Does a smile come easily, or is a frown more familiar to the person? Is the person's conversation lively and quick or are few words spoken?

7. Sense the type of profession for which the person is best suited. Remember, the person may not have selected the proper profession because of family or financial pressures.

8. As you walk to the person's home, note its color and structure. Go inside. Is the home spacious, with steps leading to other levels, or is it small and compact? Do the same for the person's second home if he or she has one. You may pick this one up stronger than the first or pick up only the second.

9. Look outside and describe the terrain. Can you see for miles, or is your vision blocked by hills or mountains? Can you feel or hear water nearby? If so, is it still, like a lake, or running like a river? Are there trees, flowers, and other plants, or only rocks and sand? Don't be afraid to pick up the soil and feel its texture. This always helps me decide if it's sandy, or a dark, rich loam, or some other soil. Look for leaves or needles on the ground to help you decide on the types of trees.

10. What hobbies or sports does the person pursue?

1. Martin

Answer found on page 163.

PERSONAL PROFILE   (Circle or fill in as appropriate)

Name _____
FIRST   MIDDLE   LAST

Colors   Number 1 color:

physical reactor   emotional reactor   mental reactor

Age   1–12   13–19   20–29   30–39   40–49   50–59   60–69   70–over

Hair   light medium dark   short medium long   thinning bald

curly wavy straight   blonde brown red black gray

Eyes   blue   green   hazel   brown

Build   tall medium short   stocky muscular   slender average heavy

small-boned medium-boned big-boned

Race   white   black   Asian   Hispanic   other

Marital Status   single   married   separated   divorced   widowed

Children   number   ages   sex

Pets   cats birds dogs horses livestock reptiles fish number_____

Personality   cheerful/happy   gregarious/outgoing   studious/serious

sense of humor   domineering/demanding   reserved/quiet

Profession   mental   emotional   physical

Residence   house condominium apartment duplex room   other_____

Description   brick   stone   siding   wood   stucco   other

Type   single floor   two-story   split-level   small   average   large

Location   mountains hill desert city town suburb country seashore forest

Vacation or second home   yes   no

Description: _____

_____

Hobbies and Sports _____

2. Annis

Answer found on page 164.

PERSONAL PROFILE   (Circle or fill in as appropriate)

*Name*_____
            FIRST   MIDDLE   LAST

Colors   Number 1 color:

physical reactor   emotional reactor   mental reactor

Age   1–12   13–19   20–29   30–39   40–49   50–59   60–69   70–over

Hair   light medium dark   short medium long   thinning bald

curly wavy straight   blonde brown red black gray

Eyes   blue   green   hazel   brown

Build   tall medium short   stocky muscular   slender average heavy

small-boned medium-boned big-boned

Race   white   black   Asian   Hispanic   other

Marital Status   single   married   separated   divorced   widowed

Children   number   ages   sex

Pets   cats birds dogs horses livestock reptiles fish number_____

Personality   cheerful/happy   gregarious/outgoing   studious/serious

sense of humor   domineering/demanding   reserved/quiet

Profession   mental   emotional   physical

Residence   house condominium apartment duplex room   other_____

Description   brick   stone   siding   wood   stucco   other

Type   single floor   two-story   split-level   small   average   large

Location   mountains hill desert city town suburb country seashore forest

Vacation or second home   yes   no

Description: _____

_____

Hobbies and Sports _____

3. Leonard

Answer found on page 165.

PERSONAL PROFILE   (Circle or fill in as appropriate)

Name_____
           FIRST   MIDDLE   LAST

Colors   Number 1 color:

   physical reactor   emotional reactor   mental reactor

Age   1–12   13–19   20–29   30–39   40–49   50–59   60–69   70–over

Hair   light   medium   dark   short   medium   long   thinning   bald

   curly   wavy   straight   blonde   brown   red   black   gray

Eyes   blue   green   hazel   brown

Build   tall   medium   short   stocky   muscular   slender   average   heavy

   small-boned   medium-boned   big-boned

Race   white   black   Asian   Hispanic   other

Marital Status   single   married   separated   divorced   widowed

Children   number   ages   sex

Pets   cats   birds   dogs   horses   livestock   reptiles   fish   number_____

Personality   cheerful/happy   gregarious/outgoing   studious/serious

   sense of humor   domineering/demanding   reserved/quiet

Profession   mental   emotional   physical

Residence   house   condominium   apartment   duplex   room   other_____

Description   brick   stone   siding   wood   stucco   other

Type   single floor   two-story   split-level   small   average   large

Location   mountains   hill   desert   city   town   suburb   country   seashore   forest

   Vacation or second home   yes   no

   Description: _____

   _____

Hobbies and Sports _____

4. Cynthia

Answer found on page 166.

PERSONAL PROFILE   (Circle or fill in as appropriate)

Name _____
FIRST   MIDDLE   LAST

Colors   Number 1 color:

physical reactor   emotional reactor   mental reactor

Age   1–12   13–19   20–29   30–39   40–49   50–59   60–69   70–over

Hair   light medium dark   short medium long   thinning bald

curly wavy straight   blonde brown red black gray

Eyes   blue   green   hazel   brown

Build   tall medium short   stocky muscular   slender average heavy

small-boned   medium-boned   big-boned

Race   white   black   Asian   Hispanic   other

Marital Status   single   married   separated   divorced   widowed

Children   number   ages   sex

Pets   cats birds dogs horses livestock reptiles fish number_____

Personality   cheerful/happy   gregarious/outgoing   studious/serious

sense of humor   domineering/demanding   reserved/quiet

Profession   mental   emotional   physical

Residence   house condominium apartment duplex room   other_____

Description   brick   stone   siding   wood   stucco   other

Type   single floor   two-story   split-level   small   average   large

Location   mountains hill desert city town suburb country seashore forest

Vacation or second home   yes   no

Description: _____

_____

Hobbies and Sports _____

96

5. **William (Bill)** *Answer found on page 167.*

PERSONAL PROFILE   (Circle or fill in as appropriate)

Name _____
              FIRST   MIDDLE   LAST

Colors   Number 1 color:

   physical reactor   emotional reactor   mental reactor

Age   1–12   13–19   20–29   30–39   40–49   50–59   60–69   70–over

Hair   light   medium   dark   short   medium   long   thinning   bald

   curly   wavy   straight   blonde   brown   red   black   gray

Eyes   blue   green   hazel   brown

Build   tall   medium   short   stocky   muscular   slender   average   heavy

   small-boned   medium-boned   big-boned

Race   white   black   Asian   Hispanic   other

Marital Status   single   married   separated   divorced   widowed

Children   number   ages   sex

Pets   cats   birds   dogs   horses   livestock   reptiles   fish   number_____

Personality   cheerful/happy   gregarious/outgoing   studious/serious

   sense of humor   domineering/demanding   reserved/quiet

Profession   mental   emotional   physical

Residence   house   condominium   apartment   duplex   room   other_____

Description   brick   stone   siding   wood   stucco   other

Type   single floor   two-story   split-level   small   average   large

Location   mountains   hill   desert   city   town   suburb   country   seashore   forest

   Vacation or second home   yes   no

   Description: _____

   _____

Hobbies and Sports _____

6. Ethel

Answer found on page 168.

PERSONAL PROFILE   (Circle or fill in as appropriate)

Name _____

        FIRST   MIDDLE   LAST

Colors   Number 1 color:

physical reactor   emotional reactor   mental reactor

Age   1–12   13–19   20–29   30–39   40–49   50–59   60–69   70–over

Hair   light medium dark   short medium long   thinning bald

       curly wavy straight   blonde brown red black gray

Eyes   blue   green   hazel   brown

Build   tall medium short   stocky muscular   slender average heavy

       small-boned medium-boned big-boned

Race   white   black   Asian   Hispanic   other

Marital Status   single   married   separated   divorced   widowed

Children   number   ages   sex

Pets   cats birds dogs horses livestock reptiles fish number_____

Personality   cheerful/happy   gregarious/outgoing   studious/serious

       sense of humor   domineering/demanding   reserved/quiet

Profession   mental   emotional   physical

Residence   house condominium apartment duplex room   other_____

Description   brick   stone   siding   wood   stucco   other

Type   single floor   two-story   split-level   small average large

Location   mountains hill desert city town suburb country seashore forest

       Vacation or second home   yes   no

       Description: _____

_____

Hobbies and Sports _____

7. Dale

Answer found on page 168.

PERSONAL PROFILE   (Circle or fill in as appropriate)

Name_____
          FIRST   MIDDLE   LAST

Colors   Number 1 color:

physical reactor   emotional reactor   mental reactor

Age   1–12   13–19   20–29   30–39   40–49   50–59   60–69   70–over

Hair   light   medium   dark   short   medium   long   thinning   bald

curly   wavy   straight   blonde   brown   red   black   gray

Eyes   blue   green   hazel   brown

Build   tall   medium   short   stocky   muscular   slender   average   heavy

small-boned   medium-boned   big-boned

Race   white   black   Asian   Hispanic   other

Marital Status   single   married   separated   divorced   widowed

Children   number   ages   sex

Pets   cats   birds   dogs   horses   livestock   reptiles   fish   number_____

Personality   cheerful/happy   gregarious/outgoing   studious/serious

sense of humor   domineering/demanding   reserved/quiet

Profession   mental   emotional   physical

Residence   house   condominium   apartment   duplex   room   other_____

Description   brick   stone   siding   wood   stucco   other

Type   single floor   two-story   split-level   small   average   large

Location   mountains   hill   desert   city   town   suburb   country   seashore   forest

Vacation or second home   yes   no

Description: _____

_____

Hobbies and Sports _____

8. *Anne Michele*

Answer found on page 169.

PERSONAL PROFILE   (Circle or fill in as appropriate)

*Name*_____
FIRST   MIDDLE   LAST

Colors   Number 1 color:

physical reactor   emotional reactor   mental reactor

Age   1–12   13–19   20–29   30–39   40–49   50–59   60–69   70–over

Hair   light medium dark   short medium long   thinning bald

curly wavy straight   blonde brown red black gray

Eyes   blue   green   hazel   brown

Build   tall medium short   stocky muscular   slender average heavy

small-boned medium-boned big-boned

Race   white   black   Asian   Hispanic   other

Marital Status   single   married   separated   divorced   widowed

Children   number   ages   sex

Pets   cats birds dogs horses livestock reptiles fish number_____

Personality   cheerful/happy   gregarious/outgoing   studious/serious

sense of humor   domineering/demanding   reserved/quiet

Profession   mental   emotional   physical

Residence   house condominium apartment duplex room   other_____

Description   brick   stone   siding   wood   stucco   other

Type   single floor   two-story   split-level   small   average   large

Location   mountains hill desert city town suburb country seashore forest

Vacation or second home   yes   no

Description: _____

_____

Hobbies and Sports _____

104

9. Ellsworth (Ted)

Answer found on page 170.

PERSONAL PROFILE   (Circle or fill in as appropriate)

*Name*_____
        FIRST   MIDDLE   LAST

Colors   Number 1 color:

physical reactor   emotional reactor   mental reactor

Age   1–12   13–19   20–29   30–39   40–49   50–59   60–69   70–over

Hair   light medium dark   short medium long   thinning bald

curly wavy straight   blonde brown red black gray

Eyes   blue   green   hazel   brown

Build   tall medium short   stocky muscular   slender average heavy

small-boned medium-boned big-boned

Race   white   black   Asian   Hispanic   other

Marital Status   single   married   separated   divorced   widowed

Children   number   ages   sex

Pets   cats birds dogs horses livestock reptiles fish number_____

Personality   cheerful/happy   gregarious/outgoing   studious/serious

sense of humor   domineering/demanding   reserved/quiet

Profession   mental   emotional   physical

Residence   house condominium apartment duplex room   other_____

Description   brick   stone   siding   wood   stucco   other

Type   single floor   two-story   split-level   small   average   large

Location   mountains hill desert city town suburb country seashore forest

Vacation or second home   yes   no

Description: _____

_____

Hobbies and Sports _____

106

10. Mark

Answer found on page 171.

PERSONAL PROFILE   (Circle or fill in as appropriate)

Name _____
FIRST   MIDDLE   LAST

Colors   Number 1 color:

physical reactor   emotional reactor   mental reactor

Age   1–12   13–19   20–29   30–39   40–49   50–59   60–69   70–over

Hair   light medium dark   short medium long   thinning bald

curly wavy straight   blonde brown red black gray

Eyes   blue   green   hazel   brown

Build   tall medium short   stocky muscular   slender average heavy

small-boned   medium-boned   big-boned

Race   white   black   Asian   Hispanic   other

Marital Status   single   married   separated   divorced   widowed

Children   number   ages   sex

Pets   cats birds dogs horses livestock reptiles fish number_____

Personality   cheerful/happy   gregarious/outgoing   studious/serious

sense of humor   domineering/demanding   reserved/quiet

Profession   mental   emotional   physical

Residence   house condominium apartment duplex room   other_____

Description   brick   stone   siding   wood   stucco   other

Type   single floor   two-story   split-level   small   average   large

Location   mountains hill desert city town suburb country seashore forest

Vacation or second home   yes   no

Description: _____

_____

Hobbies and Sports _____

TEN

What's in a Name?

*T*his exercise is a duplicate of the one in Chapter Nine, except you will not have a picture to intuit from, only a name. Although this may seem to be a greater task than the one just performed, you will actually find a name provides as much information as a picture.

In my early years of counseling, I worked only from names of people about whom my clients wished information. My clients often found it difficult to believe that I could provide that much data from just a person's name. Finally, to eliminate their doubt, I began requesting that my clients bring pictures of the people to me. The pictures made them feel more secure about the information I gave them.

Select one of the following names and ask yourself questions to decide what the person is like. The process is like reaching into a knitting basket and finding the end of a piece of yarn. As you pull it out of the basket, you find that it seems endless. So is the information you receive from your intuition as you use your intellect to describe and clarify the information. The more you pull out, the more there is that becomes visible.

Ask the same questions of each person that you did in Chapter Nine, filling out one personal profile per person. You will have to go a step further than you did in Chapter Nine, as you will be describing the person physically without the assistance of a photograph.

1. Describe the physical attributes of the person:

a) *Age*—Is the person a child, teenager, young adult, middle-aged, or older? You can start with the age of a child and gradually bring the person up to what you feel is his or her current age.

b) *Skin*—Is the skin tone fair, medium, olive, or dark? How does it compare to your skin coloring? Use yourself for comparison to the person while deciding on all physical attributes.

c) *Hair*—Does the hair feel light, or can you darken it? Starting with light hair, gradually add color until it feels right. Now reach out and touch the hair. Do you feel it is straight, smooth, wavy, curly, coarse, or fine? What length can your hands feel?

d) *Eyes*—You can try each color on the eyes until you are satisfied. I often try to picture the person as though I was looking straight into his or her eyes, and I ask myself what color is looking back at me.

e) *Build*—You can picture the person standing in front of you and decide if you must look up, down, or level when talking to him or her. If you must look up, where does your head come to on the person's body? As for the person's weight, reach out and touch an arm. Is it large or small around? Look at the face: is it thin or full? Use clues that you would normally use to judge a person's size.

2. Decide which colors are part of the person's program. Is the person a mental, emotional, or physical reactor? Which professional field seems to suit the person best?

3. What is the person's marital status? If the person has a family, how many children are in the family?

4. In what type of residence does the person live? Describe the surrounding terrain.

5. What are the person's personality traits? As in Chapter Nine, try a smile on his or her face and feel whether it stays.

Don't hesitate to add any bits of pertinent information not required for the chart. Your intellect may describe fascinating things your intuition brings up to you.

You can amaze your family and friends when they mention the name of a person unknown to you, by replying with an apt description of that stranger.

Begin by writing the name on the top of the Personal Profile. This will help you focus on that person.

NAMES

Mary Jane L.

Bruce E.

Flora M.

Alfred B.

Lisa F.

Alvy M.

Sally N.

John P.

Answers found on pages 172 through 178.

PERSONAL PROFILE   (Circle or fill in as appropriate)

*Name*_____
            FIRST   MIDDLE   LAST

Colors   Number 1 color:

    physical reactor   emotional reactor   mental reactor

Age   1–12   13–19   20–29   30–39   40–49   50–59   60–69   70–over

Hair   light medium dark   short medium long   thinning bald

    curly wavy straight   blonde brown red black gray

Eyes   blue   green   hazel   brown

Build   tall medium short   stocky muscular   slender average heavy

    small-boned medium-boned big-boned

Race   white   black   Asian   Hispanic   other

Marital Status   single   married   separated   divorced   widowed

Children   number   ages   sex

Pets   cats birds dogs horses livestock reptiles fish number_____

Personality   cheerful/happy   gregarious/outgoing   studious/serious

    sense of humor   domineering/demanding   reserved/quiet

Profession   mental   emotional   physical

Residence   house condominium apartment duplex room   other_____

Description   brick   stone   siding   wood   stucco   other

Type   single floor   two-story   split-level   small   average   large

Location   mountains hill desert city town suburb country seashore forest

    Vacation or second home   yes   no

    Description: _____

    _____

Hobbies and Sports _____

PERSONAL PROFILE   (Circle or fill in as appropriate)

Name _____
    FIRST   MIDDLE   LAST

Colors   Number 1 color:

physical reactor   emotional reactor   mental reactor

Age   1–12   13–19   20–29   30–39   40–49   50–59   60–69   70–over

Hair   light medium dark   short medium long   thinning bald

curly wavy straight   blonde brown red black gray

Eyes   blue   green   hazel   brown

Build   tall medium short   stocky muscular   slender average heavy

small-boned medium-boned big-boned

Race   white   black   Asian   Hispanic   other

Marital Status   single   married   separated   divorced   widowed

Children   number   ages   sex

Pets   cats birds dogs horses livestock reptiles fish number_____

Personality   cheerful/happy   gregarious/outgoing   studious/serious

sense of humor   domineering/demanding   reserved/quiet

Profession   mental   emotional   physical

Residence   house condominium apartment duplex room   other_____

Description   brick   stone   siding   wood   stucco   other

Type   single floor   two-story   split-level   small   average   large

Location   mountains hill desert city town suburb country seashore forest

Vacation or second home   yes   no

Description: _____

_____

Hobbies and Sports _____

PERSONAL PROFILE   (Circle or fill in as appropriate)

Name _____
         FIRST   MIDDLE   LAST

Colors   Number 1 color:

    physical reactor   emotional reactor   mental reactor

Age   1–12   13–19   20–29   30–39   40–49   50–59   60–69   70–over

Hair   light medium dark   short medium long   thinning bald

    curly wavy straight   blonde brown red black gray

Eyes   blue   green   hazel   brown

Build   tall medium short   stocky muscular   slender average heavy

    small-boned medium-boned big-boned

Race   white   black   Asian   Hispanic   other

Marital Status   single   married   separated   divorced   widowed

Children   number   ages   sex

Pets   cats birds dogs horses livestock reptiles fish number_____

Personality   cheerful/happy   gregarious/outgoing   studious/serious

    sense of humor   domineering/demanding   reserved/quiet

Profession   mental   emotional   physical

Residence   house condominium apartment duplex room   other_____

Description   brick   stone   siding   wood   stucco   other

Type   single floor   two-story   split-level   small   average   large

Location   mountains hill desert city town suburb country seashore forest

    Vacation or second home   yes   no

    Description: _____

    _____

Hobbies and Sports _____

PERSONAL PROFILE   (Circle or fill in as appropriate)

Name _____
  FIRST   MIDDLE   LAST

Colors   Number 1 color:

physical reactor   emotional reactor   mental reactor

Age   1–12   13–19   20–29   30–39   40–49   50–59   60–69   70–over

Hair   light medium dark   short medium long   thinning bald

curly wavy straight   blonde brown red black gray

Eyes   blue   green   hazel   brown

Build   tall medium short   stocky muscular   slender average heavy

small-boned medium-boned big-boned

Race   white   black   Asian   Hispanic   other

Marital Status   single   married   separated   divorced   widowed

Children   number   ages   sex

Pets   cats birds dogs horses livestock reptiles fish number_____

Personality   cheerful/happy   gregarious/outgoing   studious/serious

sense of humor   domineering/demanding   reserved/quiet

Profession   mental   emotional   physical

Residence   house condominium apartment duplex room   other_____

Description   brick   stone   siding   wood   stucco   other

Type   single floor   two-story   split-level   small   average   large

Location   mountains hill desert city town suburb country seashore forest

Vacation or second home   yes   no

Description: _____

_____

Hobbies and Sports _____

PERSONAL PROFILE   (Circle or fill in as appropriate)

Name _____
      FIRST   MIDDLE   LAST

Colors   Number 1 color:

   physical reactor   emotional reactor   mental reactor

Age   1–12   13–19   20–29   30–39   40–49   50–59   60–69   70–over

Hair   light medium dark   short medium long   thinning bald

      curly wavy straight   blonde brown red black gray

Eyes   blue   green   hazel   brown

Build   tall medium short   stocky muscular   slender average heavy

      small-boned   medium-boned   big-boned

Race   white   black   Asian   Hispanic   other

Marital Status   single   married   separated   divorced   widowed

Children   number   ages   sex

Pets   cats birds dogs horses livestock reptiles fish number_____

Personality   cheerful/happy   gregarious/outgoing   studious/serious

      sense of humor   domineering/demanding   reserved/quiet

Profession   mental   emotional   physical

Residence   house condominium apartment duplex room   other_____

Description   brick   stone   siding   wood   stucco   other

Type   single floor   two-story   split-level   small   average   large

Location   mountains hill desert city town suburb country seashore forest

      Vacation or second home   yes   no

      Description: _____

      _____

Hobbies and Sports _____

PERSONAL PROFILE   (Circle or fill in as appropriate)

Name _____
FIRST   MIDDLE   LAST

Colors   Number 1 color:

physical reactor   emotional reactor   mental reactor

Age   1–12   13–19   20–29   30–39   40–49   50–59   60–69   70–over

Hair   light medium dark   short medium long   thinning bald

curly wavy straight   blonde brown red black gray

Eyes   blue   green   hazel   brown

Build   tall medium short   stocky muscular   slender average heavy

small-boned medium-boned big-boned

Race   white   black   Asian   Hispanic   other

Marital Status   single   married   separated   divorced   widowed

Children   number   ages   sex

Pets   cats birds dogs horses livestock reptiles fish number_____

Personality   cheerful/happy   gregarious/outgoing   studious/serious

sense of humor   domineering/demanding   reserved/quiet

Profession   mental   emotional   physical

Residence   house condominium apartment duplex room   other_____

Description   brick   stone   siding   wood   stucco   other

Type   single floor   two-story   split-level   small   average   large

Location   mountains hill desert city town suburb country seashore forest

Vacation or second home   yes   no

Description: _____

_____

Hobbies and Sports _____

PERSONAL PROFILE   (Circle or fill in as appropriate)

Name_____

FIRST   MIDDLE   LAST

Colors   Number 1 color:

physical reactor   emotional reactor   mental reactor

Age   1–12   13–19   20–29   30–39   40–49   50–59   60–69   70–over

Hair   light   medium   dark   short   medium   long   thinning   bald

curly   wavy   straight   blonde   brown   red   black   gray

Eyes   blue   green   hazel   brown

Build   tall   medium   short   stocky   muscular   slender   average   heavy

small-boned   medium-boned   big-boned

Race   white   black   Asian   Hispanic   other

Marital Status   single   married   separated   divorced   widowed

Children   number   ages   sex

Pets   cats   birds   dogs   horses   livestock   reptiles   fish   number_____

Personality   cheerful/happy   gregarious/outgoing   studious/serious

sense of humor   domineering/demanding   reserved/quiet

Profession   mental   emotional   physical

Residence   house   condominium   apartment   duplex   room   other_____

Description   brick   stone   siding   wood   stucco   other

Type   single floor   two-story   split-level   small   average   large

Location   mountains   hill   desert   city   town   suburb   country   seashore   forest

Vacation or second home   yes   no

Description: _____

_____

Hobbies and Sports _____

PERSONAL PROFILE   (Circle or fill in as appropriate)

Name _____
          FIRST   MIDDLE   LAST

Colors   Number 1 color:

physical reactor   emotional reactor   mental reactor

Age   1–12   13–19   20–29   30–39   40–49   50–59   60–69   70–over

Hair   light medium dark   short medium long   thinning bald

curly wavy straight   blonde brown red black gray

Eyes   blue   green   hazel   brown

Build   tall medium short   stocky muscular   slender average heavy

small-boned   medium-boned   big-boned

Race   white   black   Asian   Hispanic   other

Marital Status   single   married   separated   divorced   widowed

Children   number   ages   sex

Pets   cats birds dogs horses livestock reptiles fish number_____

Personality   cheerful/happy   gregarious/outgoing   studious/serious

sense of humor   domineering/demanding   reserved/quiet

Profession   mental   emotional   physical

Residence   house condominium apartment duplex room   other_____

Description   brick   stone   siding   wood   stucco   other

Type   single floor   two-story   split-level   small   average   large

Location   mountains hill desert city town suburb country seashore forest

Vacation or second home   yes   no

Description: _____

_____

Hobbies and Sports _____

ELEVEN

Programs of Inanimate & Animate Objects

*Y*ou've now discovered that names and pictures give off programs, but programs don't stop there. Other objects, animate as well as inanimate, also broadcast programs. In class I normally have the students work with two objects of a similar nature, such as two necklaces. Each one gives off a different program, depending on, for example, who gave it to you, how you feel about that person, the time period when it was presented to you, and the history behind the object.

Pictured in the book are some objects you can work with on which you can immediately check the answers. The way to excel in this particular aspect of intuition is to ask friends to loan you objects with which you can practice. When using actual objects, as opposed to photographed objects, you can use your sense of touch, which will heighten the feelings you receive.

The first part of the chapter will be devoted to inanimate objects. In the second part you will have the opportunity to practice with animate objects other than humans. Some of you may question the value of sharpening your intuition on inanimate objects. This exercise not only is a way to increase your intuition but also can be used to obtain valuable information. For example, it was not unusual when my sons were teenagers for one of them to come into the house and ask me what was wrong with his car. Without any mechanical knowledge, I could sit quietly and come up with a layperson's description of what was wrong with the engine, the fuel line, or some other part of the car. My sons often laughed at my descriptions but were always able to translate them into mechanic's terminology.

When my sons and their friends were in school, they would come to me when they wanted to buy a used car. I could tell them the history of the car, whether the owner was telling the truth, and approximately how long the car would last. I was able to feel the background and future performance of the car, which saved them many headaches.

Or you can use this exercise on a contract, or on a product that you want to buy or market or in which you want to invest. You want to feel if the product is built well, if it will last, how long it is going to be on the market, and if the advertisements do the product justice.

There are many ways your intuition and intellect can be used on inanimate objects. An airplane is an inanimate object. Before a plane crash, one young college man said to his friend, "I don't want to go on this trip. I'm afraid this plane will crash," (Patrice Gaines-Carter and James Munoz, "Families Tell of Foreboding," *Washington Post*, 19 Aug. 1987, Section A1). His friend assured him they would be okay. They went ahead with the trip, and both of them died. Had these young men been taught from childhood that intuition was a valid source of information, they would have taken his feelings into serious consideration, not have gotten on that plane, and still be alive today.

I use this same sensing when working on homicide cases. It assists me in deciding whether a knife, gun, rope, club, or other type of inanimate object was used as a weapon. It helps me to look at the type of vehicles and houses involved. In one case I felt the victim was next to a mattress, but she wasn't in a house; she was in a junkyard, with a discarded mattress over her body.

INANIMATE OBJECTS

1. Where did the object originate? Was it made or purchased in the country in which you live? If so, which region? Some ways to define this is to travel the distance in your mind to the place from

where you feel the object came. Does it feel like it is from another city or state? If it does, how far do you have to travel to get there? Is it from a foreign country? Is it a neighboring one, or must you cross an ocean to get there? Do most of the people living there have black hair, as in Asia, blonde hair, as in Scandinavia, red hair, as in Ireland or Scotland, or do the people have hair of all colors? Now add the sense of hearing. Can you hear any type of accent? Is the language guttural, a romance language, or Oriental? Or does the accent belong to one of the regions of the United States?

2. Who originally purchased the item? A man, woman, girl, boy, or more than one person? This is where you use the symbol that represents man, woman, or child to you. I often look to the shape of the hand of the person making the purchase. Is it masculine, feminine, or childlike? Are the skin tones dark or light?

3. Was it a gift, purchased by its owner, or handed down as an heirloom? If a gift, was it from a friend, relative, or business associate? Is that person still living?

4. How does the owner feel about the object and the person who gave it to him or her? Remember, you are feeling what that person feels. Do you want to hold the object close to you? Did it once have importance but no longer? Do you feel affection, or anger, as though it is from a former friend, or a sense of loss, as if the giver is no longer alive?

5. Do you sense anything about previous owners, particularly in the case of heirlooms and art objects? You can pick up something as simple as the prior owner's feeling about the object or, if you want to take the time, you can even pick up a total psychological profile of that person.

6. When comparing similar objects owned by the same person, toward which object does he or she have the most emotional attachment? What are the owner's feelings toward each object? Which is his or her least favorite? Which giver has the greatest importance in his or her life? Which items were purchased by the owner?

To assist you with this exercise, I have selected some pieces of jewelry belonging to me on which you can practice.

The first picture is of two strands of pearls.

1. This necklace is 28 inches long. The clasp is a jade oval set in yellow gold.

2. This necklace is 21 inches long. Its clasp is white gold and has eight small diamonds and one larger green stone.

Answers may be found on page 178.

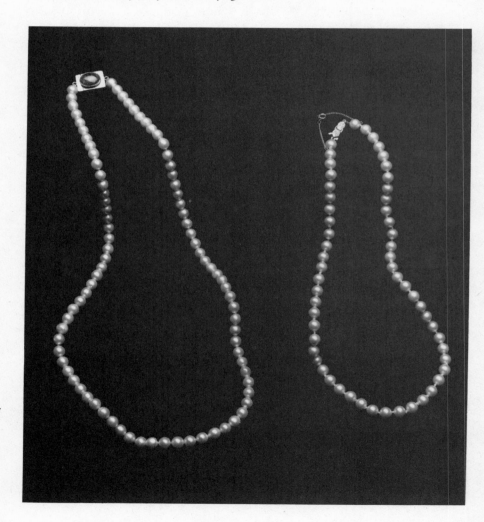

INANIMATE PROFILE

Origin

locale   native country   foreign country

received from   man   woman   girl   boy   group   relative

   friend   ancestor   company   other

Owners

Any previous owners?   How many?

Previous owner's feelings concerning object?

Present owner's feelings about object?

Present owner's feelings regarding giver of gift?

Other Notes

The second picture is of three bracelets.

1. One is a gold link bracelet. The links are florentine braids held together with smaller links decorated with tiny gold balls.

2. In the middle is a wide silver bracelet with a center stone from South America. The stone has several shades of blue and green blending together. To one side are two small turquoise stones. The center stone is held from each side by two graceful silver leaves.

3. This bracelet is made of red jade links connected with circles of gold in an Oriental motif. Even though it is designated red jade, the color is more of a golden brown.

Answers may be found on page 179.

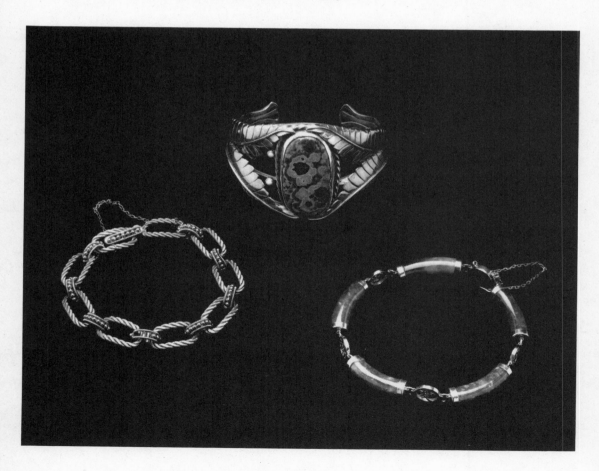

INANIMATE PROFILE

Origin

locale   native country   foreign country

received from   man   woman   girl   boy   group   relative

friend   ancestor   company   other

Owners

Any previous owners?   How many?

Previous owner's feelings concerning object?

Present owner's feelings about object?

Present owner's feelings regarding giver of gift?

Other Notes

The third picture shows three rings.

1. The face of this ring is oblong in shape. It contains twenty-two diamonds set around an emerald.

2. This ring is a rectangular ruby set with two small diamonds on each side.

3. This ring is a large, rectangular golden topaz set in platinum with six diamonds on each side. Each group of diamonds forms a flower with two leaves.

Answers may be found on page 179.

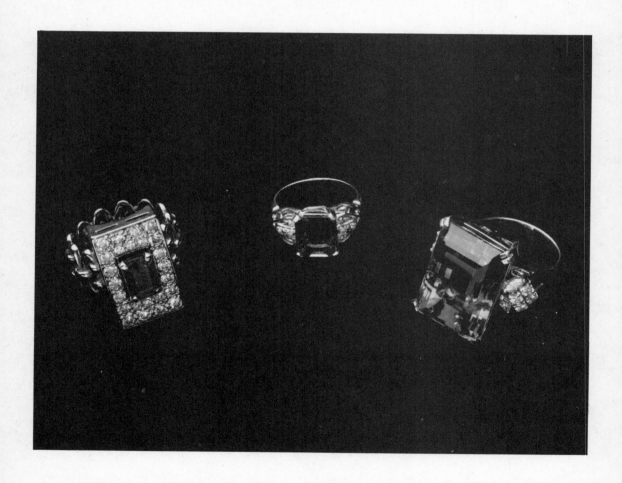

INANIMATE PROFILE

Origin

locale   native country   foreign country

received from   man   woman   girl   boy   group   relative

friend   ancestor   company   other

Owners

Any previous owners?   How many?

Previous owner's feelings concerning object?

Present owner's feelings about object?

Present owner's feelings regarding giver of gift?

Other Notes

ANIMATE OBJECTS

Now let's work with living objects that are not human beings. This exercise can also be a useful tool. It can help in anything from diagnosing an animal's health problems to locating a missing animal.

A riding instructor in California had a valuable horse that none of the veterinarians could cure. By going through that horse's feeling, from the top of his head to the tip of his tail, I intuited that certain things were lacking in the horse's digestive system and diet. With this knowledge the owner was able to give the horse certain supplements and cure him of his problems.

In a homicide case animate objects are always important. One thing I've taught myself to do if a person was last seen away from civilization is look for the types of animals in that area. This is my way of knowing in what region the body is and how far it may be from civilization. For instance, if I feel only domestic animals in the area, the body is near civilization. If I feel only wild animals, I can be assured that it is not near the city. If both are present, the body is probably on the edge of town, that is, in an area bordering on uninhabited terrain.

The senses of touch and hearing are especially important in working with animate objects. Following are some pertinent questions:

1. Does the animal have a coat of fur, feathers, or smooth skin? Reach out and touch it to get the feeling. Is it wet or dry?

2. What color is the animal? Is it light, dark, bright, or multicolored?

3. Does the animal live on the ground, in the trees, or in the water? Does the animal fly?

4. What type of sound do you hear from the animal? Does it make sound through a beak? Does it roar like a lion or meow like a cat? Is it an animal that doesn't make a noise? Is it loud or quiet?

5. Where does the animal live? Sense what its body touches. Is it dirt, rock, leaves, water, tree bark, or hay? Go ahead and feel its habitat. How does your intellect translate what you touch?

6. What is the climate where it lives? Is it cold or hot, or do the seasons alternate? Does the animal migrate? See if you can get it to travel during certain seasons.

7. What does the animal eat? Is it leaves, hay, meat, vegetables, grains, or insects? Use your sense of taste in this one. If you were chewing its food, what texture would you find?

8. Is this a domestic or wild animal? Does it live inside with other people, out in a field, or in a forest? Put people around it. Does the animal stay, run away, or attack?

You will find eight pictures of animate objects in the answer section of this book, pages 180–182. Fill out the following animate profile on each picture *prior* to turning to the pictures. This is a time when it's advantageous to have a partner who can check each picture after you finish a profile. This is an exercise you can continue to work on with pictures belonging to other people.

ANIMATE PROFILE

Type of coat

    Fur   short long   smooth fluffy coarse

    Skin   smooth scales wrinkled   wet dry   sheds skin

Color   dark   light   multicolored   bright

Domesticated   Wild

Migratory   Nonmigratory

Habitat   *Ground*   dirt rocks underground

    barn house pasture jungle

    Trees   limbs nest

    Water   ocean lake river

    other (specify, if possible)

Climate   cold mild hot seasonal

Diet   meat grains insects fruits/vegetables fish grass/hay

    other (specify, if possible)

Method of communication   chirp bark meow quack neigh

    moo roar trumpet squeak growl hiss

    other (specify, if possible)

Other Information

ANIMATE PROFILE

Type of coat

    Fur   short long   smooth fluffy coarse

    Skin   smooth scales wrinkled   wet dry   sheds skin

Color   dark light   multicolored   bright

Domesticated   **Wild**

Migratory   **Nonmigratory**

Habitat   *Ground*   dirt   rocks   underground

    barn   house   pasture   jungle

    Trees   limbs   nest

    Water   ocean lake river

    other (specify, if possible)

Climate   cold mild hot   seasonal

Diet   meat grains insects   fruits/vegetables   fish   grass/hay

    other (specify, if possible)

Method of communication   chirp bark meow quack neigh

    moo roar trumpet squeak growl hiss

    other (specify, if possible)

Other Information

ANIMATE PROFILE

Type of coat

    Fur   short long   smooth fluffy coarse

    Skin   smooth scales wrinkled   wet dry   sheds skin

Color   dark light multicolored bright

Domesticated   **Wild**

Migratory   **Nonmigratory**

Habitat   *Ground*   dirt rocks underground

    barn house pasture jungle

    Trees   limbs nest

    Water   ocean lake river

    other (specify, if possible)

Climate   cold mild hot seasonal

Diet   meat grains insects fruits/vegetables fish grass/hay

    other (specify, if possible)

Method of communication   chirp bark meow quack neigh

    moo roar trumpet squeak growl hiss

    other (specify, if possible)

Other Information

ANIMATE PROFILE

Type of coat

    Fur   short   long   smooth fluffy coarse

    Skin   smooth scales wrinkled   wet dry   sheds skin

Color   dark   light   multicolored   bright

Domesticated   *Wild*

Migratory   *Nonmigratory*

Habitat   *Ground*   dirt   rocks   underground

   barn   house   pasture   jungle

   Trees   limbs   nest

   Water   ocean   lake   river

   other   (specify, if possible)

Climate   cold   mild   hot   seasonal

Diet   meat   grains   insects   fruits/vegetables   fish   grass/hay

   other   (specify, if possible)

Method of communication   chirp   bark   meow   quack   neigh

   moo   roar   trumpet   squeak   growl   hiss

   other   (specify, if possible)

Other Information

ANIMATE PROFILE

Type of coat

Fur   short   long   smooth fluffy coarse

Skin   smooth scales wrinkled   wet dry   sheds skin

Color   dark   light   multicolored   bright

Domesticated   Wild

Migratory   Nonmigratory

Habitat   *Ground*   dirt   rocks   underground

barn   house   pasture   jungle

Trees   limbs   nest

Water   ocean   lake   river

other (specify, if possible)

Climate   cold   mild   hot   seasonal

Diet   meat   grains   insects   fruits/vegetables   fish   grass/hay

other (specify, if possible)

Method of communication   chirp   bark   meow   quack   neigh

moo   roar   trumpet   squeak   growl   hiss

other (specify, if possible)

Other Information

ANIMATE PROFILE

Type of coat

   Fur   short long   smooth fluffy coarse

   Skin   smooth scales wrinkled   wet dry   sheds skin

Color   dark light multicolored bright

Domesticated   *Wild*

Migratory   *Nonmigratory*

Habitat   *Ground*   dirt rocks underground

   barn house pasture jungle

   Trees   limbs nest

   Water   ocean lake river

   other (specify, if possible)

Climate   cold mild hot seasonal

Diet   meat grains insects fruits/vegetables fish grass/hay

   other (specify, if possible)

Method of communication   chirp bark meow quack neigh

   moo roar trumpet squeak growl hiss

   other (specify, if possible)

Other Information

ANIMATE PROFILE

Type of coat

    Fur   short long   smooth fluffy coarse

    Skin   smooth scales wrinkled   wet dry   sheds skin

Color   dark light multicolored bright

Domesticated   **Wild**

Migratory   **Nonmigratory**

Habitat   *Ground*   dirt rocks   underground

    barn house pasture jungle

    Trees   limbs nest

    Water   ocean lake river

    other (specify, if possible)

Climate   cold mild hot seasonal

Diet   meat grains insects fruits/vegetables fish grass/hay

    other (specify, if possible)

Method of communication   chirp bark meow quack neigh

    moo roar trumpet squeak growl hiss

    other (specify, if possible)

Other Information

ANIMATE PROFILE

Type of coat

    Fur   short   long   smooth fluffy coarse

    Skin   smooth scales wrinkled   wet dry   sheds skin

Color   dark   light   multicolored   bright

Domesticated   *Wild*

Migratory   *Nonmigratory*

Habitat   *Ground*   dirt rocks underground

   barn house pasture jungle

   Trees   limbs nest

   Water   ocean lake river

   other (specify, if possible)

Climate   cold mild hot seasonal

Diet   meat grains insects fruits/vegetables fish grass/hay

   other (specify, if possible)

Method of communication   chirp bark meow quack neigh

   moo roar trumpet squeak growl hiss

   other (specify, if possible)

Other Information

TWELVE

Describing Locations

*I*n this chapter you will find yourself taking mental trips to specific locations. You will be integrating your intuition with your other senses. Some of your travels will be to foreign countries, and others will be in your own land. Do not let your intellect try to decide where the location may be and whether it is familiar to you. That would be a form of guessing. It is best to set aside any preconceived thoughts about the area and start by adding one piece of information at a time until you feel you have a complete picture. You may want to have a piece of paper and pencil handy to draw any shapes that come to mind. For the physical reactors that often starts the intuition flowing.

If you have only one strong feeling about the place, such as water, stone, trees, or desert, that's fine, because it's the first step to the complete picture. Don't start to guess or use your imagination. With practice you will be able to build the entire picture in your mind. This type of exercise is discussed by Dr. Targ and Dr. Puthoff in their book *Mind Reach*. You will find reading their book helpful in carrying out this exercise.

What you want to do is describe the feeling of the area.

1. Is there a building or structure? Use your sense of touch. As you run your hand over it, does it feel smooth like metal, marble, or glass? Or does it have the texture and warmth of wood? Stand next to the building. What does the height feel like? Is it short or tall? Are there any rounded or pointed shapes? Draw any shapes that you might feel: circular, elongated, pointed, square, anything that you learned in Chapter Eight, Sensing Shapes. Now you've used your senses of sight and touch, so let's add the sense of hearing.

2. What type of activity takes place in the building, business or recreational? Is there a lot of sound, making the place seem congested with people? Are there any sounds of machinery, office equipment, or vehicles? Are there other sources of noise? Is there noise day and night, or just during specific hours?

3. Of what does the landscape consist? Can you add trees, water, mountains, or other buildings? Listen for any sounds, such as running water or rustling tree leaves. Try to select the location in the same way you selected the location of the residence of a person in a personal profile.

4. Does it feel familiar, as though it is in your country? If not, look and listen to the people of that country to see the type of clothing they wear and hear how they speak.

5. Now let's add the senses of smell and taste. Are there any particular odors associated with that location? Do you smell the exhaust of automobiles? Or the smell of the outdoors or a forest? Do you smell the sea? To all this, add the sense of taste. Try the foods of the country. Are they hot and spicy? Bland? Heavy with sauces? Is there a flavor of the Orient or do you taste the fresh fruits of an island?

Fill in your feelings of each location on the next four pages.

Answers found on pages 183 through 186.

Location One

Location Two

MIND SENSE

Location Three

Location Four

Location Five

Location Six

Location Seven

Location Eight

THIRTEEN

The Intuitive Detective

I normally follow certain steps when working on a crime. First, I do a personal profile of the victim. This enables me to understand the victim's state of mind at the time of the crime. I look to see if the person knew the suspect or not. I also determine whether the victim had any reason to feel fear prior to the incident. This tells me whether the victim had been previously threatened or was afraid of retribution for any of his or her own acts. If I decide the victim knew the suspect, I check on his or her feelings toward family members, household members, friends, and business associates. This narrows down the field to anyone among those people capable of committing the crime and whose relationship with the victim could culminate in an act of this nature. I then mentally reenact the crime to see if the person matches any of the clues pertaining to the incident. If my feeling is that the suspect was a large person, and none of the people fit the description, then it cannot be any of them. If the culprit had light hair and all of the candidates have dark hair, they are eliminated from suspicion. I also find out how they felt about the victim.

Next, I do a personal profile of the suspect, even if the detective has no suspects. If there is a suspect, the matter is much easier, as I then look to see the reason for the crime, whether the suspect had a weapon, and the type of alibi. Each of these is gone over intuitively with a fine-tooth comb, because it must be proven where the weapon originated and whether the alibi is false. I then must provide information about the suspect's actions and location. If there is no suspect, the work really begins with a physical description of the suspect, the same as in the personal profile in Chapter Nine. Before I leave the suspect, I check to see if he or she has any coconspirators and compile information on them also.

If the victim is still missing, the next step is to decide if the person is living or dead. If dead, I decide what weapon caused his or her death. I listen for the sound of a gun, and I feel for the steel of a knife, the tightening of a rope, the pressure of fingers on the neck, the sense of drowning, the sense of falling, or the impact of a blunt instrument.

The way I place the victim in his or her current location is by starting from the last time the victim was seen and checking to see if he or she is still near that location. If the victim is not, I look to see how he or she was taken away from there and what distance he or she traveled. Next, I look to see if the victim is in or near a city or around trees, water, or mountains. It's important to give a lot of detail about this. For example, I check to see if the soil is local or from another area. I often use my sense of touch and feel the soil.

I look to see if the victim is near buildings, and if so, whether they are houses, offices, or manufacturing plants. I try to describe a number of structures in the area, such as a nearby church, a white house with blue shutters, a neighborhood store, a shopping center, a construction site, a warehouse, or a manufacturing plant. If the victim is among buildings, he or she is usually easier to locate than if he or she is in an undeveloped area, such as a forest. If the area is a forest, deserted beach, or other uninhabited area, I try to locate other landmarks in the vicinity. I look for the last inhabited area the victim traveled through or anything the victim passed that stands out as being different. I check the type of highway or road used to reach the place where the victim is. Is it a dirt road, a two-lane road, or a four-lane highway? Is there a fork in the road? Is the road straight, winding, mountainous, or flat? Does it cross another major artery? In a forest all trees tend to look similar, so I can't just describe trees, though it is important to identify the leaf or needle of the trees, because it may help eliminate certain parks or places. I try to recognize any sounds, such as the sound of a sawmill, trucks for a logging operation, campers, or a highway. If I hear a highway, I listen for whether it is heavily traveled by trucks, automobiles, or both. I listen for drilling or airplanes, and if I hear a plane, I listen for whether it is a commercial or private plane. On one occasion I felt the victim was located under a main airplane pattern, because planes constantly flew overhead. Another time I was able to identify the road because of the type of truck that frequently traveled the road. I also listen for other sounds, such as rivers, wildlife, or domesticated animals—any sounds that might give me one more clue to the puzzle. In addition, I use my sense of smell. There may be a particular odor in that area, such as fresh-cut wood, an oil well, or a previous forest fire, which helps me to distinguish that area.

No matter how trivial the information may seem I write it down, because it may be the one clue that completes the puzzle. There were times when I first began working with law enforcement that I discarded some of my feelings as irrelevant, because my intellect could not assimilate them. I later discovered these bits of information were important to the detective working the case.

I have found that problems can arise if I allow my intellect to dictate what the feeling means, so I stick with the facts that I know if I can't translate everything. I learned to do this through trial and error. For example, I once worked on a case where a girl of ten or twelve had been missing for a couple of weeks. Many details were clear: a man had abducted her, raped her, and left her lying on dirt with blood around her. I was certain that after the act the man had not taken her into his house but had left her lying on the ground and returned to his home. Feeling sure of these details and knowing she had not returned home made me assume she was dead. She was not. The man had dug a large hole in his backyard, put the girl in it, and placed a cover over the opening so that she was unable to escape. My intellect assumed that because she was lying on dirt she was dead. Fortunately, the child was discovered alive by a neighbor and rescued. The man was arrested.

Another thing I don't do is try to force my intellect to understand a feeling that it cannot assimilate. One case I worked on concerned a college student who had disappeared from her summer job at Yosemite National Park. I provided the detectives with explicit details about her death, the person responsible, and the area where she could be found. While deciding where she was, I looked for wild or domestic animals, which could assist in pinpointing her location. During this process I found both types of animals attempting to reach her body, but being thwarted. I was constantly impressed that the animals circled her body. The circling motion was strong, yet I could not intellectually interpret why they were circling her. The detectives and I attempted to solve this with our intellects. They offered suggestions, such as she was under one of the manhole covers in the park. Continuing to interpret, I felt a tree trunk and wondered if she had been stuck into a log. Nothing my intuition gave me seemed to fit.

When she was discovered, it all became clear. She had been thrown from an airhole in a tunnel on a road that was high enough to overlook a camp. Her body had hit the mountain slope below the tunnel, which had catapulted her into the top branches of a tree, where animals came and circled her.

These are both examples of the fact that intuition without intellect cannot provide you with all the answers. My intellect had never experienced a body in a treetop or a child captive underground.

The first part of this exercise (pages 148 through 153) is carried out with pictures of criminals done by police artist Tom Macris and myself. Answer as many questions as possible without forcing your intuitive feelings or allowing them to be overpowered by your intellect. The second part of this exercise asks you to work from the names of the suspects and victims (pages 154 through 162). Answers may be found in Chapter Fourteen on pages 187 to 190.

Picture 1

1. What crime or crimes did this person commit—robbery, burglary, kidnapping, rape, murder, or a combination of some or all of these?

2. What was the number of victims. What were their sexes and ages?

3. What was the reason for the crime? Did the suspect know the victim? Did they have a dispute?

4. What type of weapon was used—gun, knife, blunt instrument, or hands?

5. Did the suspect use a vehicle? If so, what was the type of vehicle used by the suspect—car, truck, motorcycle, or bicycle? Was it owned by the suspect or the victim? Or was it stolen?

6. Locate the body, if there is one. In what type of terrain is it found—city, country, desert, beach, or mountains? Add every detail you can to this picture.

Other information:

Picture 2

1. What crime or crimes did this person commit—robbery, burglary, kidnapping, rape, murder, or a combination of some or all of these?

2. What was the number of victims. What were their sexes and ages?

3. What was the reason for the crime? Did the suspect know the victim? Did they have a dispute?

4. What type of weapon was used—gun, knife, blunt instrument, or hands?

5. Did the suspect use a vehicle? If so, what was the type of vehicle used by the suspect—car, truck, motorcycle, or bicycle? Was it owned by the suspect or the victim? Or was it stolen?

6. Locate the body, if there is one. In what type of terrain is it found—city, country, desert, beach, or mountains? Add every detail you can to this picture.

Other information:

Picture 3

1. What crime or crimes did this person commit—robbery, burglary, kidnapping, rape, murder, or a combination of some or all of these?

2. What was the number of victims. What were their sexes and ages?

3. What was the reason for the crime? Did the suspect know the victim? Did they have a dispute?

4. What type of weapon was used—gun, knife, blunt instrument, or hands?

5. Did the suspect use a vehicle? If so, what was the type of vehicle used by the suspect—car, truck, motorcycle, or bicycle? Was it owned by the suspect or the victim? Or was it stolen?

6. Locate the body, if there is one. In what type of terrain is it found—city, country, desert, beach, or mountains? Add every detail you can to this picture.

Other information:

DENISE R.   *Location:* Northern California
Age: Early twenties   *Hair:* Light   *Eyes:* Brown   *Build:* Average

Personal profile of victim:

1. How did she feel about her life?

      Mentally

      Emotionally

      Physically

2. Did she have any problems with

      Family members?

      Friends?

      Coworkers?

3. Did she have any fear or prior knowledge that this crime might happen?

4. Were any other victims involved?

SUSPECT OR SUSPECTS

Male   Female   How many of each?

Approximate age of each?

1. Physical details regarding each:

Hair color and style

Eye color

Skin tone

Body build

2. Personal profile of suspect or suspects:

Mental

Emotional

Physical

3. Type of:

Crime

Vehicle

Weapon

4. What was the connection to the victim?

5. What was the reason for the criminal act?

6. Describe the locations of:

Crime

Victim

7. Was the suspect or suspects apprehended?

ELROY F.   *Location:* Northern California
Age: Late thirties   *Hair:* Medium   *Eyes:* Hazel   *Build:* Average

Personal profile of victim:

1. How did he feel about his life?

   Mentally

   Emotionally

   Physically

2. Did he have any problems with

   Family members?

   Friends?

   Coworkers?

3. Did he have any fear or prior knowledge that this crime might happen?

4. Were any other victims involved?

SUSPECT OR SUSPECTS

Male   Female   How many of each?

Approximate age of each?

1. Physical details regarding each:

Hair color and style

Eye color

Skin tone

Body build

2. Personal profile of suspect or suspects:

Mental

Emotional

Physical

3. Type of:

Crime

Vehicle

Weapon

4. What was the connection to the victim?

5. What was the reason for the criminal act?

6. Describe the locations of:

Crime

Victim

7. Was the suspect or suspects apprehended?

MARY S.   **Location:** California Valley
Age: Early twenties   **Hair:** Light   **Eyes:** Light   **Build:** Petite

Personal profile of victim:

1. How did she feel about her life?

Mentally

Emotionally

Physically

2. Did she have any problems with

Family members?

Friends?

Coworkers?

3. Did she have any fear or prior knowledge that this crime might happen?

4. Were any other victims involved?

SUSPECT OR SUSPECTS

Male   Female   How many of each?

Approximate age of each?

1. Physical details regarding each:

Hair color and style

Eye color

Skin tone

Body build

2. Personal profile of suspect or suspects:

Mental

Emotional

Physical

3. Type of:

Crime

Vehicle

Weapon

4. What was the connection to the victim?

5. What was the reason for the criminal act?

6. Describe the locations of:

Crime

Victim

7. Was the suspect or suspects apprehended?

FOURTEEN

Answers

CHAPTER NINE

1. Martin

Colors He is a high receiver on the intuitive and sensitive level, and has humanitarian energy, which is his 1A area. This is combined equally with indigo, thus making this area of the mental 1B. Number 2 is his physical, which he uses to carry out his tasks.

Age Late thirties.

Hair Medium brown, straight, and medium length.

Eyes Blue.

Build Tall, medium weight.

Race Caucasian.

Marital status Married.

Children Three boys, ages two, four, and four months.

Pets None.

Residence: *description, type, location*   Brick-front, two-story house, with cream-colored siding. (You may have felt three stories because of the full basement.) A large deck on the back overlooks a stream and large wooded area. The trees are evergreen and deciduous. The house sits on a slight rise in the suburbs of one of the East Coast states. Martin has no vacation home.

Personality   Gregarious, outgoing, usually cheerful, with a sense of humor.

Profession   Education administrator/teacher. He is training for a future position as a school principal.

Hobbies and sports   Martin enjoys landscaping, building, fishing, hunting, and a good game of tennis.

2. Annis

Colors   Annis is strongest in the purple and indigo area, with a close second in the yellow and green. She uses her physical side to fulfill her tasks.

Age   Fifties.

Hair   Light brown and gray, worn medium length.

Eyes   Hazel.

Build   Tall and average weight.

Race   Caucasian.

Marital status   Married.

Children   Five, three sons and two daughters. All are college graduates. If you felt more children, you may have picked up her daughter-in-law or son-in-law, or perhaps her four grandchildren: two granddaughters and two grandsons.

Pets   You will find all types of pets around her: a large gray Persian and an orange Manx share her home, and assorted other cats live in the barn. Her dog is a gray-and-white Border collie. There are numerous horses and herds of cattle on her property.

Residence: *description, type, location* Annis lives in a house made of wood, but you may be impressed with glass, as one of the wings is a greenhouse. The main house is white and two-story and the greenhouse is on a slightly lower level. Part of the house is pre-Civil War, with exposed-log walls. You may pick up other buildings on the property, because there is a small white country store with an apartment and a large porch, a one-story studio, a two-story wooden building originally used as a kitchen, and several outbuildings. The farm is located in a wooded and mountainous area, with two fast-running streams on the property. Leading to it is an old wooden bridge and a narrow country road. Annis's second home is a two-story house in town.

Personality Cheerful and outgoing, Annis has a nice sense of humor, but when working shows her more serious side. She is extremely hospitable. You will find her home filled with guests from all parts of the world.

Profession Artist, sculptor, and art teacher at a university.

Hobbies and sports Aerobics and inspirational studies.

3. Leonard

Colors He is a rare breed in that he is equally balanced between the physical, the emotional, and the mental levels.

Age Late sixties.

Hair Medium brown turning gray, straight, short.

Eyes Hazel.

Build Tall, medium weight.

Race Caucasian.

Marital status Widowed and remarried to a woman of Chinese descent.

Children Three male stepchildren, ages fifteen to twenty-three.

Pets One German shepherd.

Residence: *description, type, location* He lives in a long single-story house of white stucco with blue trim that has a wooden deck stretching across the entire back and is set on a hillside in the suburbs, overlooking a lake. You will probably feel a great deal of foliage surrounding the house, because it sits on several acres of land on which are many types of trees, an orchard, and a garden. He has a one-story vacation home in the Arizona desert, where you will find tall cliffs and a mesa.

Personality   Leonard is one of the most gracious, kindly humanitarians I have ever met. Although he is cheerful and outgoing, with a sense of humor, you will often see the serious side of him.

Profession   Attorney. His services for low-income people are gratis.

Hobbies and sports   Gardening, inspirational writing, tennis, track, baseball, basketball, and fishing.

4. Cynthia

Colors   Indigo (the mental) is Cynthia's number 1 area, followed by the physical, number 2, and the emotional, number 3.

Age   Twenty-five to thirty.

Hair   Blonde, straight, and cut shoulder-length.

Eyes   Blue.

Build   Petite and medium weight.

Race   Caucasian.

Marital status   Married.

Children   She has a boy, age four, and a girl, age seven, both beautiful blondes.

Pets   One large brown dog named Greg, a hamster known as Cuddles, a black-and-white kitten named Sadie, and a tiger cat called Melvin.

Residence: description, type, location   She lives in a two-story house of brick with sand-colored siding and brick-red shutters, which is located in the suburbs. The deck on the back of the house overlooks a small winding stream set in forested parkland. The house also has a full basement, which may make you think the house has three floors. Her other property—four houses and one townhouse—is rental real estate. None of them is used as a second home.

Personality   Cynthia is cheerful and outgoing. She is always laughing and very sociable.

Profession   She is a registered nurse and stencils creative borders for rooms in people's homes part-time.

Hobbies and sports   Aerobics, racquetball, and antiques.

5. William (Bill)

Colors   Bill's number 1 energy is a blend of indigo and green, with touches of yellow, making him an intuitive diagnostician. His number 2 energy is red.

Age   Fifties.

Hair   Medium brown with some gray.

Eyes   Blue-gray.

Build   Average height and medium weight.

Race   Caucasian.

Marital status   Married.

Children, pets and details regarding his residence   See the description given for Annis, his wife, in picture number 2.

Personality   Bill is a warm and charming man who is interested in many aspects of life. He is outgoing, with a sense of humor. In the town where he lives, he helped start a new bank and has been active as a community leader, overseeing the building of a shopping center, and has also been a senate candidate for his state.

Profession   Medical doctor.

Hobbies and sports   Bill raises cattle. He spends a lot of free time buying, raising, and trading horses. His friends affectionately call him "the horse trader." He also enjoys buying and trading antiques, and gardening. For relaxation, he plays the guitar with the rest of the musical members in his family.

6. Ethel

Colors Ethel's number 1 color is humanitarian. Number 2 is a mental color, which she uses in her work, and number 3 is a physical color.

Age Fifties.

Hair Medium brown.

Eyes Hazel.

Build Short and slender.

Race Caucasian.

Marital status Married.

Children Ethel has two girls and one boy, ranging in ages from twenty-seven to thirty.

Pets Two residents are feline.

Residence: *description, type, location* Her home is a yellow wooden house with brown trim. It is a medium-sized two-story house located in the California mountains. There is no second home.

Personality Although Ethel has a serious and quiet side, you will find her friendly and outgoing, with a sense of humor.

Profession She is a deputy sheriff, held in high regard.

Hobbies and sports Ethel is an avid reader. She also likes photography, sewing, aerobics, and jogging.

7. Dale

Colors In his work as an architect, Dale calls on a blend of indigo, 1A, and red, 1B, which are complemented by the green and yellow area as number 2.

Age Early sixties.

Hair Gray.

Eyes Green.

Build Average and stocky.

Race   Caucasian.

Marital status   Married.

Children   Three boys, aged thirty-one to thirty-seven.

Pets   Dale has a black Doberman named Satin. Two other previous pets that were important were Jac, a Great Dane, and Harvey, a big, fluffy, gray cat.

Residence: description, type, location   His house sits on a hill overlooking the San Francisco Bay and the Golden Gate Bridge. It's made of brown wood, and has extensive panels of glass. Sitting under a eucalyptus tree in the back yard is a redwood hot tub, which Dale frequently uses after a game of tennis. Dale has a second home, a 108-year-old wooden triplex.

Personality   Dale has a sense of humor and has never met a stranger. When planning one of the many buildings he designs, you will find him on the serious side.

Profession   Architect.

Hobbies and sports   Dale enjoys sculpting and painting. You will also find him at home on the tennis court or golf course, as well as hovering over a pool table.

8. Anne Michele

Colors   Her great depth of emotion makes the humanitarian, yellow-green, number 1, which she uses with children and animals. Her mental, indigo, is number 2, followed by her physical, red, which is number 3.

Age   Late teens.

Hair   Blonde and wavy, worn medium-length.

Eyes   Large and blue.

Build   Slender and of average height.

Race   Caucasian.

Marital status   Single.

Children   None.

Pets   A poodle and a thoroughbred horse named Woody.

Residence: *description, type, location*   Her number 1 house is a two-story home of gray brick with white trim, located on the outskirts of a city, where the forest meets the bay. Other residences you may pick up around Anne Michele are a large brick apartment house in an East Coast city where her mother resides, or her dormitory at a southern university, which is also brick.

Personality   She is reserved, quiet, studious, and serious, but also has a sense of humor.

Profession   At the moment she is registered as an engineering student, but has decided to change her major to humanities next semester.

Hobbies and sports   She plays soccer, squash, and field hockey, and competes as an equestrian.

9. Ellsworth (Ted)

Colors   Ted uses his indigo and blue first, with his emotional a close second. His physical is third.

Age   Late thirties.

Hair   Very blonde, straight, and short.

Eyes   Blue.

Build   Average height and slender.

Race   Caucasian.

Marital status   Married.
He shares the children, pets, a residence, and real estate with Cynthia, number 4.

Personality   Ted can be serious at work, but is usually cheerful and happy. He is endowed with a sense of humor.

Profession   Medical doctor, specializing in radiology. You may feel his uniform, which is that of a Navy doctor and officer. Although Ted and Bill are both medical doctors, you should have felt distinct psychological differences between them.

Hobbies and sports Ted is interested in antiques, genealogy, and reading. He spends time reading the stories gravestones tell. He also plays golf and jogs.

10. Mark

Colors Mark's 1A color is indigo (mental), his 1B color is red (physical). His emotional area is second.

Age Late teens.

Hair Blonde, medium length, and wavy.

Eyes Blue.

Build Average height and muscular.

Race Caucasian.

Marital status Single.

Children None.

Pets Yin and Yang, two Abyssinian cats, and a black Doberman named Kelly.

Residence: *description, type, location* He lives in a large red brick colonial house with gray pillar and shutters, which is located in the suburbs of Maryland. The house sits on a knoll overlooking ninety-five acres of forest. His second residence is a room on the second floor of a large brick dormitory at the University of Maryland.

Personality Though Mark is in the honors program and a member of MENSA, you're rarely aware of his serious and studious side because he usually shows his outgoing, happy, and humorous side.

Profession He is a student of engineering and aerospace. His summer profession has been to the work for the United States Park Services at the Custis Lee Mansion in Arlington Cemetery.

Hobbies and sports Creating on computers, science literature, football, wrestling, weight lifting, track, and soccer.

CHAPTER TEN

1. Mary Jane L.

Colors Her 1A color is a blend of green and yellow, and her 1B color is a blend of indigo and purple. Number 2 is her physical.

Age Sixties.

Hair Medium length, light brown, and curly.

Eyes Hazel.

Build Slender, average height.

Race Caucasian.

Marital status Divorced.

Children Four girls and one boy, all between thirty and thirty-eight. Two of the girls are twins.

Pets None, but the day I spoke to her about this book three cats called on her.

Residence: description, type, location She lives in a condominium in a town near the foothills of the Blue Ridge Mountains. It is a single-floor wooden structure of medium size. Her second residence is a condominium in a large brick building located in a nearby city.

Personality She is considerate, kind, and intelligent. She is reserved and has a quiet manner.

Profession Family and corporate clinical psychologist. She has spent the past few years working for the federal government.

Hobbies and sports Gardening, walking, traveling, and a great deal of reading.

2. Bruce E.

Colors Bruce is a combination of indigo as number 1, emotional as 2A and physical as 2B.

Age Early thirties.

Hair   Curly red, average length.

Eyes   Blue.

Build   Slender, average height.

Race   Caucasian.

Marital status   Single.

Children   None.

Pets   One German shepherd.

Residence: description, type, location   He lives in an apartment in New York City. No second home.

Personality   He has a delightful sense of humor and usually displays a cheerful, happy mood. Sometimes, but not often, Bruce is quiet and serious.

Profession   Broker of commercial real estate.

Hobbies and sports   You may intuit other things about Bruce, such as his father is a medical doctor, and his mother recently died. You may also feel a great deal of air travel or airplanes; his sister is a flight attendant. If ballet occurred to you, it's because his older brother dances professionally in Europe. If a swimming pool or house on a hill were among your feelings, it was the California home in which he was raised.

3. Flora M.

Colors   Indigo is 1, physical is 2, and green is 3.

Age   Sixties.

Hair   Black, straight, and exceedingly long, worn in a bun.

Eyes   Brown.

Build   Petite, slender, and short.

Race   Asian.

Marital status   Married.

Children   She has three sons, between the ages of thirty and forty. One of them is a medical doctor.

Pets   One Chihuahua.

Residence: *description, type, location*   She lives is a medium-sized, one-level wooden house, located in the bustling Northern California Silicon Valley. You may see her in a large, two-story, cream-colored stucco building on a tree-lined street, which is where her business is located.

Personality   Flora always has a cheerful word for everyone. Her serious side is lightened with an acute sense of humor.

Profession   She is a fashion designer. Her physical endurance always amazes me.

Hobbies and sports   She has a great interest in music.

4. Alfred B.

Colors   His humanitarian area is the strongest, followed by physical expression, and then mental expression.

Age   Forties.

Hair   Dark brown, wavy, and medium length.

Eyes   Hazel.

Build   Average height, muscular.

Race   Caucasian.

Marital status   Married.

Children   He has two little girls, ages 2 and 3½.

Pets   A large German shepherd and a charcoal-colored cat.

Residence: *description, type, location*   He lives in a large two-story house of brick and wood, which sits on a hill in the Oregon suburbs. There are large oak trees in the yard. You can see a river from the yard. His second home is a wooden two-story condominium in a coastal city of California.

Personality   With friends Al is happy and outgoing. Among strangers he is quiet and reserved.

Profession   He is a member of the Secret Service, and is special agent in charge of his district. He was previously stationed in Santa Barbara, so you may have felt the United States president near him.

Hobbies and sports   Fishing, weight-training, and golf. He hates flying.

5. Lisa F.

Colors   Mental comes first, followed by the emotions, and then the physical.

Age   Twenties.

Hair   Medium brown, worn curly and medium-length.

Eyes   Hazel.

Build   Average height, medium weight.

Race   Caucasian.

Marital status   Married.

Children   Six-month-old baby boy.

Pets   She has two dogs, one a chow and the other a 118-pound Alaskan malamute.

Residence: *description, type, location*   Lisa lives in a three-story wooden house located in the Colorado mountains. She has no second home, but you may feel two other locations important in her life. One is Lake Tahoe, where she grew up, and the other is the Arizona desert, where she attended the university.

Personality   Her general demeanor is quiet and reserved, but she also has a happy nature and a sense of humor.

Profession   She previously worked with an electronics firm, where she used her college studies in math and computer science.

Hobbies and sports   Ballet, swimming, bicycling, and skiing on snow and water.

6. Alvy M.

Colors His number 1 color is the green and yellow area, with indigo as 2A and physical as 2B.

Age Sixties.

Hair Medium brown, straight.

Eyes Hazel.

Build Average height, medium weight.

Race Caucasian.

Marital status Married.

Children He has one son and two daughters, ranging from middle twenties to early thirties.

Pets At last report there were nine cats—mother, father, and seven little ones. Don't be surprised if Amos looms large here. He was a wonderful mongrel dog with long ears of gray, white, and black. He liked to climb the tree in the back yard and is now in dog heaven.

Residence: description, type, location His home is located in a Southern California valley near a city. It is made of brick, stucco, and wood. It is a large, L-shaped, single-floor house with a Spanish porch around the back. A high privacy fence is in the back yard. There is no second residence.

Personality The first thing you feel about Alvy is his gregarious, outgoing personality. He's blessed with a sense of humor that keeps everyone laughing.

Profession Film and television actor and producer. You may recognize Alvy as the county surveyor, Hank Kimball in the television show *Green Acres*.

Hobbies and sports Photography, cooking, and charity golf tournaments.

7. Sally N.

Colors Her number 1 color is a deep indigo, her number 2 color is green, and her number 3 color is physical.

Age   Early thirties.

Hair   Very long, dark brown, and straight.

Eyes   Hazel.

Build   Tall, medium weight.

Race   Caucasian.

Marital status   Divorced.

Children   None.

Pets   The only pets at Sally's home swim in a bowl.

Residence: description, type, location   Her home is a medium-sized two-story house made of wood and siding, and located in the suburbs. Her second home is a family vacation house located in Maine. It is made of wood.

Personality   She is friendly and outgoing, with a delightful sense of humor. She is comfortable with all types of people, because she grew up in an Air Force family, living all over the world.

Profession   She is currently a construction supervisor, training for the position of vice president of a large residential developer. She has been in all aspects of the field, from sales and marketing to the supervising of the actual construction of the homes.

Hobbies and sports   Bicycling, water skiing, swimming, aerobics, and jogging.

8. John P.

Colors   Physical is his number 1 color, mental is his number 2 color, and emotional is his number 3 color.

Age   Thirties.

Hair   Medium brown, straight.

Eyes   Brown.

Build   Large, big-boned, and extremely muscular.

Race   Caucasian.

Marital status   Divorced.

Children   One daughter in her late teens.

Pets   None.

Residence: *description, type, location*   He lives in a two-story wooden condominium in a Northern California city. There is no second residence.

Personality   John has a serious nature, with a quiet sense of humor, but is outwardly sociable.

Profession   He is an Olympic medal winner in discus throwing, and coach of a track and field department at a well-known university.

CHAPTER ELEVEN

Inanimate Objects

Picture 1

The 28-inch length of pearls was given to me by my maid of honor on the occasion of my marriage. Although purchased in Virginia, the pearls originated in the Orient, so you may get the feeling of more than one location. The gold-and-jade clasp was purchased a year later by my former husband during a trip to Bangkok. This could give you the feeling of a man and woman connected to this object. It is an excellent example of why you should take your time examining the feelings related to the object. With two people involved with this necklace, you may have experienced one program stronger than the other, or that one had been connected to the piece longer than the other. Also, you should have detected a difference in my relationship with each of these people. This necklace has always been a favorite of mine.

The shorter strand of pearls was purchased in Europe by the same former husband during a time when we were experiencing difficulties in the marriage. I seldom wear them, and feel no close attachment to them.

Picture 2

The gold link bracelet pictured here came from one of the Bahamian Islands, purchased by a male friend of Dutch descent. Things you might feel are the facts that the giver had an accent, was extremely tall, flew his own plane, owned a company in Florida, and was killed in a plane crash. The bracelet could give you feelings of both happiness and sadness. You may feel something is missing from the original piece because at one time it held two charms: a Dutch shoe and a Virgo sign. You may pick up the water, sand, soil, or palm trees of Florida, or symbols of Holland. So you see, many details can be included in one object, with all of them being intuitively true.

The silver bracelet was made by a goldsmith friend of mine. He presented it to me while I was in California. The stone is from South America. Against my skin color silver always looks cold, so I seldom wear it. The bracelet could cause you to think of South America, California, or Nevada, where the goldsmith lived. I received this bracelet following my divorce. Though I seldom wear it, I enjoy its beauty.

The red jade bracelet was a birthday present from a California attorney I used to date. It came from China and was purchased in San Francisco. If you also sensed a female connected with this bracelet, it would be my daughter, who assisted in its selection. Although I enjoy the bracelet's beauty, the relationship was short and is no longer of importance.

Picture 3

The diamond-and-emerald ring should give you a warm and special feeling. It has long been one of my favorite rings. It's an original design from New York, into which the emerald was later incorporated. The ring was my selection, but the emerald was purchased by my former husband when he was in the Orient. The emerald was formerly set in a gold ring with four diamonds on each side before I had it mounted in this ring—this could give you the feeling of both rings. This piece could also have several other feelings attached to it: the feeling of the designer, the feeling of my former husband, the feeling of the Orient, and the feeling of Virginia, where the ring was purchased.

The ruby ring was given to my mother by my father when I was a girl. It was purchased in Las Vegas, Nevada, when it was just a small town. She wore it until she died, in Arizona. The ring holds two feelings for me: one of the love I have for my father and the other of the strained relationship I had with my mother. The major feeling should be that of my mother, because she wore it all the time, but you may pick up Father's program. Mother was a short woman with reddish hair, with whom I was never close. My father was a tall, soft-spoken Texan with gray hair.

The topaz ring was purchased in Tokyo by myself, but I find I seldom wear it. You should find little emotional attachment, but you might pick up television, because I bought it when I was in Japan doing a television show. I worked on several law enforcement cases in Japan, so you may even find that as a connection.

Animate Objects

Pictures listed in order

1. African elephant

2. South American crowned crane

3. Bengal Tiger

4. Dog

5. Mother and baby seal

6. Horses

7. Alligator hatching from egg

8. Orangutan

CHAPTER TWELVE

1. Eiffel Tower

2. Pyramids

3. Capitol Building

4. Big Ben

5. Colosseum

6. Statue of Liberty

7. Golden Gate Bridge

8. Brandenburg Gate

CHAPTER THIRTEEN

Picture 1

This is a case of two small girls, ages 4 and 5, who were kidnapped, raped, and then strangled to death by the suspect and an accomplice. The suspect did not know the victims, and had picked them up in town, where they had been playing. He was known to use alcohol and drugs, which contributed to his becoming a mass murderer. The vehicle used was a pickup truck. The bodies of the girls were at the base of a low-railinged cement bridge, nude and buried in sand. There were underbrush and small trees near the scene.

One of the interesting aspects of this case was that a boyfriend of the older sister of one of the girls said he felt they were in the area where they were later located. He took a group of young people to that area and found a barrette which belonged to one of the missing girls. His intuition caused him to be a suspect for a while. The suspect in the picture was later apprehended and held in a Texas jail, where he has confessed to more than one hundred killings. When brought back to the scene of the crime, his guilt was confirmed when he went directly to the location where he had buried the girls.

As I was describing the suspect prior to his identification, one of the facial features that stood out was that he had a problem with one eye and therefore depended solely on the other eye for vision. It was later discovered that the murderer had one glass eye.

Picture 2

This was a case of a number of rapes without a known murder attached. The suspect worked alone, and the exact number of victims at this point is undetermined. The weapon was sometimes a knife from the victim's kitchen and in other cases the suspect stated that he also had a gun. Though a vehicle was never seen, it was believed that he had one, because the rapes were carried out over a large area, from San Francisco to Palo Alto. He was a stranger to his victims and was referred to as the Black Bra Rapist because during a crime he would request that the victim put on pieces of colored underwear that he selected from her bureau.

A twist in this case came after Tom Macris had finished the

drawing and we were talking to the detectives on the case. I suddenly felt Tom should add a striped T-shirt to the drawing. I had forgotten this until a detective from another city came in to talk about this suspect. When he read a description from the latest victim of what her assailant wore, it included the striped shirt. And when this same detective presented our drawing to a male witness who had seen the suspect clearly the night of the crime, his comment was that the woman who described the criminal had certainly gotten a good look at him!

Picture 3

This case was that of a young man found shot dead beside his car in the middle of a residential street. It was near a city on the water, so you may have picked up ships, a harbor, or houses. The crime was solved when a witness related what had happened. It seems the victim's car had barely bumped the car of the killer while turning a corner. When it was disclosed who the culprit was, his mug shot matched our drawing. This is another case of drugs removing all sense of compassion and responsibility in the suspect while he committed a crime.

Victim 1   Denise R.

What I found with the personal profile of Denise R. was that she felt confused on the mental level concerning a relationship. She normally responded on the emotional level in a friendly and outgoing manner, but I found that she had been feeling low. I also sensed that she had gone through a hysterical experience concerning the person connected to her disappearance, whom I felt was a man to whom she had recently broken her engagement. She had felt no fear until just prior to the crime taking place. There were no other victims involved.

The suspect's personal profile produced the following: he was fairly intelligent, mixed up emotionally, and capable of physical abuse. His hair was blonde, eyes blue, race Caucasian, and build large. The vehicle used was a rented van. The cause of death was blows to the body. The crime took place in a deserted area with a sandy beach. The suspect has been apprehended and faces charges of murder in the first degree.

Victim 2   Elroy F.

On the mental level Elroy F. was direct and to the point, not inclined to lie. On the emotional level, he was a compassionate person. He enjoyed doing things physically. He would put up with things for a long time, then would flatly say it was all over. The feeling just before he was killed was, How did I get myself into this mess? There were no other victims involved.

The female suspect, the victim's wife, had brown hair and light eyes and was of average build. Her mental level was basic. Emotionally she felt injustice about life and physically showed a great deal of anger. She was thirty-six at the time she murdered her husband. The vehicle used was a dark blue, four-door Fiat. On the weekend of the crime, they were at their summer cabin on a private, windy dirt road that led back to several cabins in foothills. A stream ran between the road and the cabin.

The perpetrator killed the victim with a gun, then proceeded to saw up his body and attempt to burn it in the fireplace. When this failed she began to bury the different pieces in the yard surrounding the cabin. She has been sentenced for her crime.

Victim 3   Mary S.

Mary S. was a very intelligent, warm, and humanitarian young woman attending college. She enjoyed physical activities. Her family was very close and caring about people. She had no idea that the crime would occur. The second victim was the man she steadily dated.

One of the suspects was a psychopath with a sadistic streak. He was thirty-three, with brown hair and an average build. He was accompanied by his pregnant wife, who drove the car. She was a green-eyed blonde of petite build who came from an upper middle-class family. It was later established that she had driven the vehicle on several occasions when he raped and killed other victims.

The two victims were abducted while leaving a college dance in a large city. The were driven a short distance out of town, where the young man was shot, killed, and left beside the road. Mary was then driven farther up into the foothills, where she was raped, killed, and left in a cul-de-sac where homes were yet to be built. The suspect and his wife then drove to the next state and caught a plane to yet another state. They were apprehended, returned, and received their sentence for the crime.

About the Author

Kathlyn Rhea has been a professional in the field of parapsychology since 1966. In 1979 her clairvoyant abilities enabled her to lead the sheriff's department to the body of a Calaveras County man missing for four months. A flurry of publicity followed. She subsequently appeared on "Evening Magazine," "That's Incredible," and "The Merv Griffin Show."

Before her interest in parapsychology, Kathlyn Rhea was a model, the founding director of Charm Associates, a modeling and fashion school in Virginia. For years she hosted a successful television talk show, "Coffee with Kay," in Florida.

Kathlyn Rhea believes that intuition is an inherent ability in us all, needing only to be nurtured and disciplined, just as any other talent does. She has been consulted on everything from building sites, personnel, product development, and financing to the stock market and the commodities market. In addition, she has aided physicians in the treatment of their patients' ailments and assisted various law enforcement agencies in their search for criminals.

PERSONAL PROFILE   (Circle or fill in as appropriate)

Name _____
       FIRST   MIDDLE   LAST

Colors   Number 1 color:

    physical reactor   emotional reactor   mental reactor

Age   1–12   13–19   20–29   30–39   40–49   50–59   60–69   70–over

Hair   light medium dark   short medium long   thinning bald

    curly wavy straight   blonde brown red black gray

Eyes   blue   green   hazel   brown

Build   tall medium short   stocky muscular   slender average heavy

    small-boned medium-boned big-boned

Race   white   black   Asian   Hispanic   other

Marital Status   single   married   separated   divorced   widowed

Children   number   ages   sex

Pets   cats birds dogs horses livestock reptiles fish number_____

Personality   cheerful/happy   gregarious/outgoing   studious/serious

    sense of humor   domineering/demanding   reserved/quiet

Profession   mental   emotional   physical

Residence   house condominium apartment duplex room   other_____

Description   brick   stone   siding   wood   stucco   other

Type   single floor   two-story   split-level   small   average   large

Location   mountains hill desert city town suburb country seashore forest

    Vacation or second home   yes   no

    Description: _____

    _____

Hobbies and Sports _____

PERSONAL PROFILE   (Circle or fill in as appropriate)

Name _____
FIRST   MIDDLE   LAST

Colors   Number 1 color:

physical reactor   emotional reactor   mental reactor

Age   1–12   13–19   20–29   30–39   40–49   50–59   60–69   70–over

Hair   light medium dark   short medium long   thinning bald

curly wavy straight   blonde brown red black gray

Eyes   blue   green   hazel   brown

Build   tall medium short   stocky muscular   slender average heavy

small-boned   medium-boned   big-boned

Race   white   black   Asian   Hispanic   other

Marital Status   single   married   separated   divorced   widowed

Children   number   ages   sex

Pets   cats birds dogs horses livestock reptiles fish number_____

Personality   cheerful/happy   gregarious/outgoing   studious/serious

sense of humor   domineering/demanding   reserved/quiet

Profession   mental   emotional   physical

Residence   house condominium apartment duplex room   other_____

Description   brick   stone   siding   wood   stucco   other

Type   single floor   two-story   split-level   small   average   large

Location   mountains hill desert city town suburb country seashore forest

Vacation or second home   yes   no

Description: _____

_____

Hobbies and Sports _____

PERSONAL PROFILE   (Circle or fill in as appropriate)

Name _____
         FIRST   MIDDLE   LAST

Colors   Number 1 color:

physical reactor   emotional reactor   mental reactor

Age   1–12   13–19   20–29   30–39   40–49   50–59   60–69   70–over

Hair   light   medium   dark   short   medium   long   thinning   bald

curly   wavy   straight   blonde   brown   red   black   gray

Eyes   blue   green   hazel   brown

Build   tall   medium   short   stocky   muscular   slender   average   heavy

small-boned   medium-boned   big-boned

Race   white   black   Asian   Hispanic   other

Marital Status   single   married   separated   divorced   widowed

Children   number   ages   sex

Pets   cats   birds   dogs   horses   livestock   reptiles   fish   number _____

Personality   cheerful/happy   gregarious/outgoing   studious/serious

sense of humor   domineering/demanding   reserved/quiet

Profession   mental   emotional   physical

Residence   house   condominium   apartment   duplex   room   other _____

Description   brick   stone   siding   wood   stucco   other

Type   single floor   two-story   split-level   small   average   large

Location   mountains   hill   desert   city   town   suburb   country   seashore   forest

Vacation or second home   yes   no

Description: _____

_____

Hobbies and Sports _____

PERSONAL PROFILE   (Circle or fill in as appropriate)

*Name*_____
          FIRST   MIDDLE   LAST

Colors   Number 1 color:

   physical reactor   emotional reactor   mental reactor

Age   1–12   13–19   20–29   30–39   40–49   50–59   60–69   70–over

Hair   light medium dark   short medium long   thinning bald

   curly wavy straight   blonde brown red black gray

Eyes   blue   green   hazel   brown

Build   tall medium short   stocky muscular   slender average heavy

   small-boned   medium-boned   big-boned

Race   white   black   Asian   Hispanic   other

Marital Status   single   married   separated   divorced   widowed

Children   number   ages   sex

Pets   cats birds dogs horses livestock reptiles fish number_____

Personality   cheerful/happy   gregarious/outgoing   studious/serious

   sense of humor   domineering/demanding   reserved/quiet

Profession   mental   emotional   physical

Residence   house condominium apartment duplex room   other_____

Description   brick   stone   siding   wood   stucco   other

Type   single floor   two-story   split-level   small   average   large

Location   mountains hill desert city town suburb country seashore forest

   Vacation or second home   yes   no

   Description: _____

   _____

Hobbies and Sports _____

ANIMATE PROFILE

Type of coat

    Fur   short   long   smooth fluffy coarse

    Skin   smooth scales wrinkled   wet dry   sheds skin

Color   dark   light   multicolored   bright

Domesticated   *Wild*

Migratory   *Nonmigratory*

Habitat   *Ground*   dirt   rocks   underground

    barn   house   pasture   jungle

    Trees   limbs   nest

    Water   ocean   lake   river

    other (specify, if possible)

Climate   cold   mild   hot   seasonal

Diet   meat   grains   insects   fruits/vegetables   fish   grass/hay

    other (specify, if possible)

Method of communication   chirp   bark   meow   quack   neigh

    moo   roar   trumpet   squeak   growl   hiss

    other (specify, if possible)

Other Information

ANIMATE PROFILE

Type of coat

Fur   short   long   smooth fluffy coarse

Skin   smooth scales wrinkled   wet dry   sheds skin

Color   dark   light   multicolored   bright

Domesticated   Wild

Migratory   Nonmigratory

Habitat   *Ground*   dirt   rocks   underground

barn   house   pasture   jungle

Trees   limbs   nest

Water   ocean   lake   river

other   (specify, if possible)

Climate   cold   mild   hot   seasonal

Diet   meat   grains   insects   fruits/vegetables   fish   grass/hay

other   (specify, if possible)

Method of communication   chirp   bark   meow   quack   neigh

moo   roar   trumpet   squeak   growl   hiss

other   (specify, if possible)

Other Information